To Andie, keep the faith! :)

FIVE AND TWENTY

[signature]

1

FIVE AND TWENTY

An NYPD Cop Story

by

Robbin Ramos

C&D Publishing Direct

New York

FIVE AND TWENTY

An NYPD Cop Story

Published by:

C&D Publishing Direct

P.O. Box 1109

Scarsdale, New York 10583

FIRST EDITION

Cover design by David Collins of Cover Creator UK

ISBN: (paperback): 978-0-9997761-2-4

ISBN: (E-book): 978-0-9997761-3-1

FIVE AND TWENTY

ONE

March 16, 1999.

Bronx In-Tactical Unit (IN-TAC), 49th PCT

1800 hours (6 pm)

It was an exceptionally cold day, even for March, and the heater in the police van wasn't working.

The three of us were headed back from the Police Academy building, located in downtown Manhattan, having made a few hundred dummy rounds for the fake yellow-barrel revolvers used for training sessions at the 49th precinct in the Bronx. I looked at my wristwatch. Six o'clock.

The Lieutenant who ran the show at IN-TAC had expected us back about an hour earlier, but none of us had ever used the machine that made the noisy-but-harmless .38 caliber blanks, and nobody at the PA seemed interested in giving us any assistance beyond wheeling the medieval device out into the hallway and wishing us luck. Besides, we would have nothing to do once we got back to the Four-Nine other than watch videos in the upstairs office until the end of the tour. During days when there were no cops from Bronx commands shipped off to the 49th precinct for training, IN-TAC was basically Romper Room. It was a shame that the detail was only a temporary assignment,

1

because in two weeks I would be returning to the 46th precinct for uniform patrol, my home since wearing the gray Academy shirt only two years earlier.

While the bulky vehicle was marked with the traditional royal blue and white colors of the NYPD, we were dressed in civilian clothing. Generally, IN-TACers would play perpetrators in the training scenarios, so it wasn't necessary to wear uniforms during our one month stay, another reason to enjoy the detail. No heavy gun belt, no sweaty, bullet-resistant vest. Just show up with your shield and identification card, and you were more than equipped. Still, I had my backup gun, a .38 revolver, in a fanny pack around my waist, but that might have been considered excessive. Most veterans would leave their guns in their lockers for the month. My service pistol, a Smith & Wesson 9mm, was in a locked box at home.

I barely knew the two guys in the van. The driver, Randy, was a veteran from PSA 8, a Housing District, whom I only had a brief conversation with. He was a short Irish guy in his thirties, a little on the heavy side, with brown hair and a serious look. The other cop's name was Ray; very fit, curly dark hair, stylish eyeglasses and an olive Italian complexion. He was in his twenties, and he had more time on the job than I did, but not necessarily more experience. He worked at the 45th precinct, a quiet house located in the Throggs Neck area of the Bronx, an area with very little crime. But like most work environments, seniority equaled respect, and I was the baby of the trio. So, I kept my mouth shut and my eyes and ears open. That was an unwritten rule new guys followed if they had any common sense at all.

We were stuck in traffic on the Cross Bronx Expressway, heading uptown. There was no need to turn on the turret lights - we weren't in a rush, and not looking to draw attention to ourselves. Ray had our only police radio, and he was listening to a situation involving the search for a missing patrolman. He'd been flipping through frequencies and, like tuning into a movie already in progress, some of the details of the search weren't clear. I'd been splitting my attention between the radio and Randy when my beeper vibrated weakly in my pocket.

Someone at my real house was paging me. I still lived with my parents, in the same small room that I had grown up in since I was eight years old. I had just turned twenty-six, in late January. I turned on my cellular phone and dialed my parents' number. My mother picked up.

"Hi, Mom. It's Chris. What's up?"

"Is everything okay?" she asked, with genuine concern in her voice. "There were cops at the house looking for you."

"What? I'm fine. Who was at the house? Guys I know?"

"I don't think so," she answered, still sounding nervous. "They said that there was a cop missing in the Bronx, and that maybe it was you. Hold on... Your father talked to them. I'll put him on."

Already, what she told me didn't make sense. My father got on the line.

3

"You all right, son?"

Despite my better judgment, I was becoming angry. There was no reason to scare my family. "Yeah, I'm fine... Did you get a name or see a shield?"

"One of them told me his name, but I honestly don't remember it. I saw his shield, though...."

"What did it look like?"

"It was gold - round with points. Sorry... I didn't get the number."

Either a Detective's or a Lieutenant's shield, I thought to myself as both designs look similar, especially to a civilian's eye. My father drove a school bus for a living, and I was the first cop in our family. The first thing that popped into my head was the Sick Desk had made an error and thought that I had called in sick. It was department policy that a sick police officer must always be home. Cops assigned to the Sick Desk would make random visits, just to check. If they didn't find you home, you'd better have a good explanation, or you're in trouble.

"Did they say what division they were from?" I asked my father, steaming. Mom probably feared the worst, I thought to myself.

"No, they didn't. There were two of them, undercover guys. The one with the gold shield - it was on a chain around his neck - asked to speak to you. They didn't tell us what it was about, but they told us not to worry, that everything was okay."

4

"Bullshit," I replied.

"I know," Dad echoed. "I didn't buy it. I followed them outside — without your mother — and asked them again what was up. They said something about a cop being missing, but that I shouldn't worry, that it probably wasn't you. He gave me a number for you to call when I got in touch with you." He read the number, and I copied it down on a piece of scrap paper. Both cops in the van with me were listening to my end of the conversation quietly, with obvious interest. The expressway around us had finally begun to open up, and Randy had the van moving at highway speed.

"I'm going to call this number and ream this guy out," I told my father, still fuming. "Anyway, tell Mom everything's fine. I'll talk to you tonight."

Even though I told my father that everything was fine, it still made no sense whatsoever. If the Sick Desk was indeed looking for me, I would have been very easy to locate. If they had my name, then they'd also have my permanent command. They could simply call the 46th precinct to find out where I was that day. The supervisor at the Four-Six would look through the roll call and find "IN-TAC" printed next to my name. Thus, the absurdity of their visit continued to rattle around my head as I dialed the number that my father had given me on my cell phone.

Nothing but a busy signal. I tried again. No answer, and no voice mail.

"Got a random visit to your house?" Randy asked, steering the van off the Castle Hill exit and onto city streets. We were about ten minutes away from the Four-Nine.

"Yeah... To see if I was home. They scared the shit out of my parents."

"I'm not surprised," Randy responded, matter-of-factly. "Believe me, the department is legendary for administrative fuck-ups."

"What precinct do you live in?" Ray interjected, still with his ear to the radio.

"Yours," I answered, referring to the 45th.

"Well, if it's any consolation, they're looking for a missing cop in the 45th. Maybe they have a list of people, and somehow your name found its way on it."

Suddenly, a weird thought weaseled its way into my mind. It was so ridiculous that I almost laughed out loud.

"Y'know... I took a drug test about a month ago. I hope it doesn't have anything to do with that. I have civilian friends who smoke pot. I hope I didn't get a contact high or something."

Recently, I had given hair samples as part of my end-of-probation medical exam and hadn't thought twice about it, until that moment.

But Ray quickly jumped to my defense.

"Don't be ridiculous. Do you have any idea how many concerts I've been to, with guys blowing shit all

6

around me? You can't pop a positive like that. You're being paranoid."

"When did you piss?" Randy asked.

"February 26th... but I gave hair. It was my end-of-probation dole exam."

"How the hell did YOU give hair?" Randy asked me incredulously, a wide smile on his face. He was referring to my clean-shaven head. It was a new style that I had recently embraced, because my hair had been thinning out on top. Of course, I wanted to rock the goatee as well, but department regulations forbade it.

Jokingly, I pulled down the collar on my shirt to reveal a forest of chest hair.

"Unfortunately, I have it everywhere except where it counts," I said.

"Well, don't worry," Randy continued. "If you had a positive result, you would have been notified in days, not weeks. Believe me, you'd already know."

He's right, I thought to myself, breathing a sigh of relief. Already, I had signed off on my background investigation, officially ending my two-year probation. It was one of the major stepping stones in every cop's career. My next hurdle would be the first hash mark, a royal blue patch sewn onto my uniform sleeve, signifying a minimum of five years of service. Casually, I shelved all thoughts of tests and drugs and hair samples, returning to my previous angry mode, as I began to plan exactly what I would say to the stupid officers who had disrupted my happy home.

I dialed the number again, but to no avail.

Busy signal.

I had no idea that my life was about to change forever.

TWO

Growing up, I never imagined that I would become a police officer.

Some guys dream about wearing a uniform, arresting "bad guys."

To be honest, I have always thought of myself as, well, a wimp.

Don't get me wrong. I've always been a bit of a peacemaker - like breaking up fights in school - and I enjoy physical sports, like football and boxing. However, I'd always avoid real confrontations, especially ones that had any chance of turning serious. You see, boxing is regulated, with a referee that can stop the fight. In a dark alley, there are no rules. I never wanted any part of the real thing, usually finding a way to talk my way out of it, a skill that ironically became quite useful in my future profession. As a cop, they teach you that your mouth is your best weapon, because it can keep you from using deadly force.

But I'm getting ahead of myself.

For as long as I can remember, I wanted to become a lawyer. I earned a college degree at age twenty, graduating with honors. Then, I attended law school, but dropped out after only one semester.

Back then, I expected everything to come easy. Honestly, I thought that I was going to become some legal

9

crusader like I'd seen in movies, battling injustice inside a courtroom. Within a year, I wound up delivering pizza. Plus, my high school sweetheart was suddenly getting married — to someone else — and that didn't exactly aid my ability to concentrate on academics.

So, I wrote the law school a fancy resignation letter and wandered off without any plan for the future.

One night after a shift at the pizzeria, I went to a friend's house for a visit. It was the spring of 1996, and I was twenty-three.

My friend Fred, also twenty-something and still living at home, ran his basement of their house almost like a community center. Guys and girls from the neighborhood would come and go at all hours of the night to drink and smoke and avoid sleep for as long as humanly possible. His mother upstairs ruled the house with a spongy fist, content that even if her 'kids' might be doing things that they shouldn't, at least they had all grown up into working adults.

Just off from his own shift at a different pizza restaurant, Fred was watching sports highlights and smoking pot from a plastic bong. He offered me some, but I said no. Occasionally, I smoked pot back then, but I had recently quit because I was overweight. Inspired by my ex's recent wedding, I decided to go on a health kick. For those of you that may be unaware, marijuana - besides making you feel high - gives you an uncontrollable urge to eat the entire refrigerator, including the handles on the door.

On his coffee table, I remember seeing a blue piece of paper with typed print. I picked it up for a closer look.

It was an order form of some kind. There were empty boxes for personal information, and on top was the seal of the City of New York.

"What's this?"

"It's an application to become a cop. There's a test this summer. I'm thinking of taking it."

"You want to be a cop?" I asked, a little surprised.

"It's a good job," Fred replied, shrugging his shoulders. "You start out with thirty thousand a year, and after five years, you're making fifty. Plus full benefits. And you retire after only twenty years. Imagine that... I'd be only forty-three years old and retired."

"Is there a college requirement?"

"Sixty credits, or two years in the military. I have plenty of time. They don't call you right away. I know a guy who took the fireman's test and they called him six years later. By the time they call me, I'll be ready."

"Not a bad idea," I told him, impressed. Suddenly, I conjured an image of my friend in that dark blue uniform, and it made me proud. I'd also get a PBA card every year, I joked to myself.

"Do you have your score back yet?" Fred asked, changing the subject.

"Not yet. They said next week." He was referring to my recent attempt to join the United States Air Force. My father, who had served in the USAF during Vietnam, was now nudging me towards a career in the military. Since I had a college degree, they told me that I could start out as an officer. However, I was still required to pass a written exam. My father was excited about it, telling me that it was a good way of life, that I could travel the world. Honestly, I liked the idea, but refused to consider it a possibility until I knew my test results.

"You'll pass," he said, smiling. "Wouldn't that be cool? You, a Lieutenant in the Air Force and me, a New York City cop? Outrageous."

With that, I sat back in silence, thinking carefully about my friend's latest plan. Thirty thousand dollars to start. Retired in twenty years, when other poor slobs have to work until sixty-two years old.

It sounded to me like Fred might be on to something.

The next morning, I drove out to the post office, filled out an application for myself, and mailed it away.

***

It was a Saturday morning in the summer, and the long line of people stretched completely around the building. Luckily for everyone, it was both warm and dry.

Only one week after my visit to the post office, I had received a letter with a test date, directing me to go to Theodore Roosevelt High School in the Bronx to take the police exam. Ironically, Fred was probably still sleeping that morning. He had gotten a sauce stain on his application while filling it out, wanted to get a clean one, and never got around to it. As I stood in line waiting patiently, I was silently amazed at the huge turnout. Tall and short, skinny and fat, every gender and race under the rainbow - all there, chatting about their personal lives with strangers, waiting with No. 2 pencils and picture IDs. I wondered how many would end up becoming cops. Looking down at my own pencil, I asked myself if I was in the right place.

I wasn't sure, but taking the test couldn't hurt. So, I continued to wait.

Eventually, they herded us into small, dingy classrooms, into old, graffitied desk chairs with dried chewing gum stuck underneath the tables. The class wasn't led by a teacher, but by a cop in full uniform. *If police officers were to moonlight as teachers, there might be less of a discipline problem in the school system*, I joked to myself. Anyway, relatively speaking, it was an easy day. Before I knew it, I was driving home, stashing the whole experience into a quiet corner of my mind, not expecting to hear from the NYPD for years, if at all. I had heard horror stories of "freezes," when the city stops hiring due to a fiscal crisis and an entire list of names meets an early grave.

I hadn't even come up with an idea for my next career plan when I got another letter in the mail. According to the city, they wanted me to take a medical exam. It said that I should arrive in business attire at six-thirty in the morning, and expect to be at their office for about four hours. While I was flattered by the quick notification, I was still a little uneasy about it all. The fantasy was all too quickly becoming a reality.

About one hundred applicants was called in for 'medicals' on that date. The address was One Lefrak City, in Queens. We all sat in a large room on the sixteenth floor, the layout much like an auditorium overlooking a oversized bay window, with a view of nothing but blue sky and white clouds. While seated, we weren't allowed to talk, forced to sit up straight and not move. Between our impressions of stone statues, we filled out tons of paperwork, mostly release forms that absolved the city of any responsibility for anything we could do that could warrant a future lawsuit. Fighting the boredom, I do remember one bright spot: A black detective who carried himself like a stand-up comedian, taking advantage of the captive audience. However, overall, it wasn't a pleasant experience.

Also, it didn't last four hours, as advertised. When I looked at the clock in my car afterwards, it was nearly seven PM - a tedious twelve-hour day.

Upon arriving home, I peeled off my suit and dropped the package of paperwork that was given to me on the kitchen table. Thankfully, I had passed their preliminary tests, as the envelope included a list of steps that I would be required to undertake, including another written test about a month down the road.

14

But I wasn't interested in any of that just yet. I needed some time to think.

Did I actually want this? This new adventure, if completed successfully, was going to require an enormous amount of effort on my part.

Lying in bed, I finally understood their game. Obviously, the NYPD was not looking for rocket scientists. They were looking for people that genuinely wanted to be cops, men and women willing to jump through hoops of fire to get the job. The true test that day was to see how many applicants would lose their minds and just walk out.

Anyway, I didn't want this to become another 'law school.' Either I would make the decision to dedicate myself for the long haul, or I'd throw the package in the kitchen away and never look back. Also, I'd already failed the Air Force exam - by only two points - but I did have the option to take it again in the future.

Staring up at the ceiling fan, the blades were spinning into a blur that resembled my situation. *Do I really want this? Should I just wait? Take the Air Force test again in six months? Keep delivering pizza?*

Eventually, the blur defined itself, and it all became clear.

The Police Department had already given me an envelope, with a schedule.

The door was open and waiting, even if only enough to wedge my foot inside.

15

I decided to push my way through.

***

There was crust in my eyes as I sipped warm coffee that early April morning in 1997, riding the train. It was almost a year after that fateful conversation with Fred regarding that piece of blue paper, about his impressive plan.

For me, his plan had become reality.

I had been accepted into the New York City Police Academy, along with twelve hundred other recruits for six months of training. That morning, I was heading to York College in Queens, a temporary site for our orientation. I was both excited and terrified, the two emotions battling for pole position.

Like cattle in business attire, we lined up outside the college campus in mock attention, single-file, not allowed to move. It was freezing that morning, still the memory of a brutal winter fresh in my mind. I didn't bring a coat with me, because I didn't own a classy-looking jacket. My hands, curled up into balls at my sides, were tingling in pain from the harsh wind that blanketed the area. Again, I began to question my motives. *Why was I standing on that*

16

damn line? I asked myself. It would have been easy enough to mark it down as just another failed experiment and go home.

It was at that moment that I began molding a personal pep-talk. It was still raw and needed refinement, but it would eventually become my mind's most powerful rallying cry. I would use it many times in the future, especially during difficult moments on patrol. It was my justification, my reason for the unreasonable, the purpose behind it all.

Five and Twenty.

I had just turned twenty-four years old. If I endured the cold and stayed in formation and did what was asked of me from that day onward, I would earn fifty thousand dollars per year in just five years, at twenty-nine years old. And at a young forty-four, I would retire. Twenty years total.

My father, a man who had tortured himself for more than sixty hours per week for decades to give my family a decent life, didn't earn that kind of money until he was well into his forties.

Five and Twenty.

So, I stayed.

Regardless of what happened to me, it was the right decision, and I will always believe that.

***

I first met John D'Angelo at a friend's house, during a college football game. A mutual friend, Robert, was having a small get-together for the championship. We were not formally introduced, so I didn't even know his name at that point. He sat quietly, nursing a beer, just content to fade into the background.

It was almost two years later when we bumped into each other again, this time at York College. It was during a short break, after we had been led into a large auditorium and to assigned seats. We recognized each other immediately and shook hands, trading hellos. It was comforting to see a familiar face in a sea of anonymous suits, and I can only assume that he felt the same, as we became the other person's shadow for the remainder of our three days on the campus grounds.

I remember noticing a troubled look on his face, as if he had carried a weight on his tremendous shoulders, but I just assumed that nerves were to blame.

Soon, I would find out the real reason.

Speaking of size, John was a big guy. Not especially tall, but extremely wide. His suit, which was probably specially tailored to fit him, still looked tight. He had a thick face that swallowed his small hazel eyes, no mustache, and brown hair in a tight buzz cut. From his appearance and tone of voice, one might have believed that John was dim-witted, but even a short conversation would dispel that notion. He was as sharp as a tack.

On our second day, I found John in a bathroom during a break. When I stood beside him to use the urinal, he looked around to see if we were alone.

"I don't know if I can do this," he said to me. His words were choked with stress.

"Of course you can," I told him.

"We're going to be late. I'll talk to you during lunch." As promised, he found me later in the cafeteria and led me to a secluded table in a far corner. We sat with our trays of food, alone.

"I didn't expect to be here," John whispered, making sure no one could hear. "I had a very high list number. They called me a week ago to take all my tests. It was a crash course."

My tuna sandwich tasted like wet cardboard, so I put it down. "Why are you telling me this?"

"I haven't told anyone else. But I need to talk about it."

He needed me to listen, not interrupt, so I kept quiet.

"I smoked pot while away at college," he finally said.

John dropped his head into his hands and continued. "I didn't expect to get called for this class. My list number is really high. They called me just last week, I did all the tests in fast forward — the run, the interviews, everything - and they took my hair five days ago. I keep thinking that, at any moment, they're gonna pull me out of the group."

"How long ago did you smoke?" I asked him, thinking carefully about the process. I knew that each application was handled differently. In my case, I had given hair samples about a month earlier, and had heard nothing. In 1997, they took two clumps of hair from the back of my head. I could have opted for an additional sample, to be locked away and tested if I disputed their findings. I declined because they were butchering people with an electric razor and leaving unflattering holes.

"Three months ago," he told me, regarding his error in judgment.

"Well, that is close. But honestly, I don't think you should be worried," I told him. During the application process, I had heard rumors that the hair test could detect the presence of marijuana for seven years or longer, so I did some homework. At that time, the NYPD took hair samples to test for the presence of illegal substances only twice in a cop's career - once during the application process, and then again at the two-year mark, the final step in escaping probation. However, at any point, they could also randomly send you to Lefrak City again and make you piss in a cup. Marijuana only shows up in urine for five to seven days, so the department was considering switching to hair testing exclusively. I continued talking.

"The hair test they use only goes back about sixty days."

He gave me a quizzical look. "Are you sure? I thought the test went back years and years."

Obviously, he had heard the same rumors that I did. "Am I sure? No. But I did a little research because I smoked pot three years ago. Actually, there are hair tests that go back that far, but not the test that the police department gives. The test they give us only goes back about thirty days. Sixty... tops."

"My father is on the job," he told me, unconvinced. "He would drop dead if I were to dole out. I can't do that to him. If I leave now, maybe I could take the next written exam..."

"Listen, I can't tell you what to do," I said, feeling uneasy. Unlike other city jobs where they send you to rehab if you 'dole' out, the NYPD had a zero-tolerance policy regarding drug use. Besides, we weren't even cops yet. "But look around you. There are twelve hundred guys here. That's a lot of hair tests. They can go back as far as they want - depending on the length of the piece of hair. The longer it is, the further back they go. But the further they go, the more money each individual test costs. Urine tests are cheaper - but pot only shows up in urine for a week. Thirty days is an eternity by comparison."

"How can you be sure?" he asked me, now poking at his pasta with a fork. I could see his big shoulders lighten up a bit.

21

"I'm not," I replied, trying to be diplomatic. "But I think they probably would've told you already."

"I hope so," John said, now eating with gusto. We sat silently for a long while, before he spoke again.

"You're a good friend, Chris," he said, with sincerity. "Thank you."

I remained quiet, only smiling back. Suddenly, I was overcome with an intense feeling of dread.

It was not every day that I was allowed to play God with someone else's career.

**

The Academy building was designed very much like any city high school, except for its odd dimensions. It was narrow and tall, squeezed tightly between other lofty structures on the east side of downtown Manhattan. The hallways and rooms were like any college setting - corridors with pastel-colored tiles, rooms with chalkboards and pull-down view screens. The only real difference between the Academy and most other schools wasn't the building itself, but the high level of discipline. Unlike Roosevelt High, you'd be hard pressed to find a single piece of bubble gum in a garbage can, much less under a table or chair.

I remember sitting quietly in one such classroom on the third floor, alongside twenty-eight other recruits in business attire, at the end of my orientation week. Still, we were not required to wear our Academy uniforms yet, a variation on the navy blue NYPD outfit but with a gray shirt. Our Academy class was broken up into forty groups - or companies - of approximately thirty students each. As fate would dictate, John and I ended up being in the same company. He had decided to risk it and stay, and heard nothing. No one pulled him out of our group, and no one ever would.

Unlike myself, John retired a police officer after twenty years of honorable service to the city.

Our schedule that day was to sit and hear speeches from faculty members on various topics, ranging from expectations while in training to actual future police work. Near the end of the day, we were visited by a female detective, dressed in a light blue business jacket and matching slacks. She was Hispanic, with long, curly dark hair and dark eyes. She carried herself with extreme confidence that presumably came from her experience as a cop. Her name isn't important as I would never see her again, but her message, which I didn't understand at the time, would one day ring with such profound truth that I still shudder at the mere memory of her.

"Every one of you here already has an identity," she said to us, sitting cross-legged on the desk in the front of the room. "Don't expect a gun or a shield to give you one. You are who you are. If you're a geek, then you'll still be a geek with a gun and a shield. Remember that."

Her comment got a chuckle from the group. I laughed, thinking that I understood her point. Looking back, I realize now that I had no clue. Next, she motioned to a recruit sitting closest to the entrance to the room.

"Officer - please close that door."

The detective wanted privacy for her next statement, as the advice she was about to give could not be found anywhere in the Patrol Guide.

"I tell you this because anyone in this room - anyone - can get 'jammed up'... Even me."

I wasn't sure what "jammed up" meant, but she followed with an explanation. "One day, you could be out on patrol, doing the right thing. Trying to be the best cop that you can be. And out of nowhere, they can come and take your gun and your shield away from you. It happens every day."

Her next comment took complete control of the class. If anyone had been daydreaming up to that point, nap time was over.

"You might be taking police action someday, forced to make a split-second decision in the heat of the moment – in good faith — and then have to spend months or even years trying to justify that decision. Or, believe it or not, you don't actually have to do anything wrong. You could simply be in the wrong place at the wrong time. They will suspend you, they will take away your toys and fire you, without hesitation. And nothing you've done in your career up to that point will matter. Therefore, if you allow a gun or a shield to become your identity, and they take them away, you'll have nothing left... ."

Unfortunately, sitting in that chair, her words were already beyond my comprehension.

At that point, it was inconceivable to me that I could ever be in a situation that my job would be in jeopardy. Of course I wasn't a saint, but I had always tried to take the correct path in life, to think things through from all angles and choose wisely. In retrospect, I was still a child at heart, a boy in a man's body who believed that life was fair, that people always get what they deserve. The wise words of an adult who had sat in my chair as a young recruit, an experienced officer who knew first-hand of cops from her own Academy class who had fallen from grace undeservingly, were brushed aside.

Worse yet, a new identity was already taking shape, merging with the preexisting one without my knowledge or control. Even if I had been a wimp, the sense of accomplishment that I was feeling just from being selected to sit in that chair had granted me a sense of confidence - even arrogance - that I had never known before.

But like all foolish children, I would have to learn the hard way.

THREE

March 16, 1999.

Bronx In-Tactical Unit. 49th PCT.

2015 hours (8:15pm)

When we returned with the police van to the second floor of the 49th precinct where the IN-TAC office was located, no one had noticed us missing. I had hoped that the mystery cops had called, which would've shed some light on the house visit, but the Lieutenant was also in the dark.

"No one called for you here," the Lieu said, a thin man in his forties with a bushy mustache and glasses. "Did you do anything stupid with the van?" He was referring to an extra trip that I had taken at around two o'clock, when I used the vehicle to go on a food run.

"Absolutely not, Lieu. I got the Mickey D's and came right back." Actually, that was a white lie. I had also made a pit stop at my house to sit on the toilet. My private residence was located in the 45th precinct, which bordered the Four-Nine. *Did I knock a side-view mirror off a parked car and not realize it?* I considered going downstairs to check the van for body damage, but then decided against it. The vehicle already had too many bumps and bruises to count, and it would prove nothing. Besides, I knew I was grasping at straws.

26

After putting the metal coffee cans filled with dummy rounds into a storage closet, I found an office telephone. I picked up the receiver and dialed the 46th precinct. A veteran cop I had worked with once before answered the phone. I asked him if anyone had called the desk, looking for me.

"Nope. Not on the four-to-twelve," he said, referring to the third platoon, which worked from four P.M. to midnight. "How's IN-TAC treating you?"

"Fun," I answered. "The highlight of my day is watching soap operas."

"I thought you were going to midnights? What happened?"

"I did for a little while," I replied, referring to my recent switch to the graveyard shift at the precinct. "I wanted to work with Ordonez, but they put me in the wrong squad. Then 'Cookie' called me from IN-TAC and asked if I wanted to be a criminal for a month. Who could refuse that?"

'Cookie' was a nickname for a female cop from the Four-Six that was assigned to IN-TAC. It was time for her to return home, so she began making phone calls to find a replacement, to hold her spot. Conveniently, she found me.

"Not many," he said in agreement. "Anyway, see you soon."

Next, I dialed the number that my father had given me. Again, no answer.

Having run out of options, I decided to just let it go. If someone was still looking, they would eventually find me, and there was no reason to worry about crossing a bridge that I couldn't even find. Besides, there was a study group going on, which was more than enough of a distraction. With a sergeant's exam on the calendar, five ambitious cops were poring over their patrol guides, shooting questions and answers back and forth at each other. Purposely, I sat on the fringe of the circle, listening to every question, silently guessing at some of the answers. It was a long way off for me, but I was already looking forward to my turn.

Eventually, it was sign out time. I found my name on the roll call sheet, quickly scratching out my initials and the time. Twenty-one hundred hours, or nine PM. It was a clear night, but still chilly. My car was parked across the street on Eastchester Road, facing the service road of the highway that I would use to get to my girlfriend's house, who was making me dinner. Everything seemed normal, identical to many other evenings.

I said my good-byes and crossed the street, got in my vehicle, and sped off.

But there was one small difference.

They were already outside, waiting for me.

I drove for only about twenty seconds before I noticed an unmarked police car in my rear-view mirror, a bright spinning turret light on its dashboard, the universal sign to either stop or get the hell out of the way.

Finally, I thought to myself, somewhat relieved. *Time to get to the bottom of this nonsense.*

I pulled over, rolled down my windows and turned off the engine, sticking both hands out the driver's side window. Since I was armed, I wanted no misunderstandings. I noticed then that there were actually two police cars, with four plainclothes cops total.

Two of them approached my side of the car, cautiously. The older of the duo had a shield hanging from a chain around his neck. It was gold, with points.

"Robbin?" The Lieutenant asked me, using my real first name. Cops that were friends knew to call me 'Chris,' by my middle name.

Obviously, these guys knew me either from a roll call, or some other kind of list.

"Yes?" I responded, wondering what I had done to warrant all that attention. *Did an angry husband make some kind of allegation against me?*

"Do you have your gun with you?" he asked me, calmly.

"May I see an ID card, Lieutenant?" I asked him, as a precaution. It was easy to get a fake shield, but it would be much harder to replicate an NYPD identification card.

He motioned to the officer next to him, who pulled out his silver patrolman's shield, identical to mine, around his neck by a chain but concealed under his shirt until then.

On the reverse side was his card in a clear plastic holder. It had his name, his shield number, and the division that he worked for.

It said "IAB."

"IAB" stood for the Internal Affairs Bureau.

IAB doesn't concern itself with civilians.

They only arrest dirty cops.

"Yes I do, sir," I said, referring to my gun, growing nervous. "In my pouch."

I began to unzip the fanny pack around my waist, assuming that they wanted to inspect my firearm. The Lieu quickly interrupted.

"Please, let me do that," he said.

I put my hands on my head and let the boss reach inside my vehicle and unzip the pouch, pulling out my stainless steel .38 caliber Smith & Wesson revolver. It disappeared from sight, as if it had never existed.

Suddenly, a phrase that had been imprinted on my brain ever since my Academy days emerged from my subconscious. I heard myself saying the words, like a recording.

"Sir... Am I the subject of an investigation?"

Unfortunately, the Lieutenant was prepared for that question. If he had said "yes," then my next words would likely have been: "Then I would like a PBA representative present before we go any further."

"Don't worry about that," he responded, calm and fast, like a telemarketer. "And please, don't speak. We just want the opportunity to talk to you. If you'll allow it, I'd like to have a sergeant sit next to you. You'll drive to where he tells you, and you'll just listen to what we have to say... Fair enough?"

With his smooth reply, I was halted in my tracks. I wanted to cooperate, so that I wouldn't somehow escalate whatever trouble I had unknowingly stumbled into. A third cop made his way from the second police vehicle to the passenger side of my car, waiting for my approval to open the door and sit down. I gave the okay, and he got in.

"Sir?" I said to the Lieutenant, my mind racing. "Please tell me what this is about."

"You had a problem with your dole test," he said, nonchalantly. "But please, don't speak. It's not the end of the world. Just listen to what the sergeant has to say first."

That fucking dole test.

I had predicted it, in the van.

Obviously, I had somehow developed a trace of marijuana in my system, probably from airborne smoke. Of course, I thought I had been careful. If I had been hanging out with civilian friends while off-duty and they wanted to smoke pot, they would either switch rooms out of courtesy for my profession, or I would leave. However, I could still

31

remember a few smoke-filled rooms during poker games, times when I had probably lingered, shaken hands with acquaintances, or listened to music a little too long.

Your fault, I repeated in my mind over and over, scolding myself as I watched the Lieu return to his squad car. *No one's fucking fault but yours, and yours alone.* I put the car in gear and followed the directions of the supervisor sitting next to me.

The sergeant in the passenger seat was a short white male, bald except for dark horseshoe hair on the sides of his head. He spoke in a soft manner, leading me to a quiet spot on the opposite side of the 1-95 service road. We were in clear view of an above-ground train station, the final stop of the Number Six line that ran north/south through the Bronx and Manhattan, all the way to the Brooklyn Bridge.

Coincidentally, I had ridden that train many times with Officer D'Angelo, dressed in our gray Academy uniforms, in the beginning.

Somehow, it seemed fitting that it might also be the location for the end.

I pulled over as the Lieutenant parked directly behind me. Exiting his unmarked patrol car, The Lieu again returned to my side, crouching down and leaning against my door, talking to me through the rolled down window. He reiterated himself about his desire for me to stay calm and just listen to what they had to say.

Of course, I felt an intense desire to defend myself, even though I already knew that my words would have no impact on what would happen. Zero-tolerance drug policy.

My police journey was over, and I knew it.

I began to feel a heavy sadness fall on my shoulders like a net, trapping and smothering me, but from the inside.

"Sir," I interrupted, pleading. "I know that this is going to be very hard for you to believe, but I didn't smoke pot. There has to be some other explanation to account for this."

"I'm sure you're right," he said, trying to keep me calm and focused. Then he continued, and made a casual statement that literally obliterated my grip on reality.

At that moment, I had to seriously question if I was awake or still asleep in bed, having a dream that had turned into an impossible nightmare.

Stunned by a single word, I wondered if this was all some kind of hoax, brought on by friends at the precinct. Honestly, I waited patiently to wake up, to hear the alarm clock buzzer, so that I could hit snooze and get another ten minutes of sleep.

But this was indeed happening, and it was fate that was making the joke, but at my expense.

The word was "cocaine."

FOUR

97–20.

The designation for my company at the Academy.

"97" refers to the year, 1997.

We were twentieth of forty companies, the last group in "A" squad. Because the building couldn't accommodate twelve hundred people all at once, our class was split into two squads, of six hundred each. The two squads would alternate schedules—five days of 7 A.M. to 3 P.M. shifts, and then the following week would consist of 3 P.M. to 11 P.M. tours, with Saturdays and Sundays off. Personally, I liked the mornings better. It was difficult to leave the house in the dark, but ending the workday in sunlight as recruits were just arriving for the beginning of their tours made dealing with Mr. Sandman worthwhile.

In the beginning, I would drive my car to the train station in Pelham Bay, at the end of the Six line. Half asleep, I would climb the steps to the platform and board an empty, quiet train. During the fifty-minute ride that would descend beneath the city, the car would fill to capacity as I would stand in my new costume and receive curious stares, like I was a fake cop on Halloween. In exchange for riding free, a city employee was told to stand to allow paying customers the opportunity to sit. Of course, the rule was broken occasionally, but a majority of the time I stood in half-empty cars, my bag on the floor between my legs, hanging onto a pole for balance. I did not want to find out

34

later that I had denied a Captain's wife a seat - or the Captain herself - dressed innocently in civilian clothing.

At my stop, I would emerge from the hole in the ground onto quiet Manhattan streets. The Academy was still a good half-mile walk from the subway exit, and I would stumble along, hoping that I had enough time for a cup of coffee. While the streets were quiet, they weren't empty. A few steps ahead, a few feet behind, across the street and all around, they walked with me in silence. With numbers steadily increasing, people all dressed like clones, dragging large black duffel bags exactly like mine, joined in a quest for a career and pension plan.

The 'muster deck' was our mutual destination. The Academy building was designed so that a large section of the third floor above the gymnasium was outdoors and exposed to the elements. We would enter the building, stop to salute the American flag, and ascend to the deck area by stairs. Of course, there was an elevator, but recruits were forbidden to use it. Many veteran cops on a trip back to the Academy look forward to their first return to the building, even if only to ride the elevator and smile about days past, and the many thousands of steps.

Once on the deck, I'd find my company and stand in formation. Soon, an instructor - usually a sergeant - would call the entire squad to attention. We would endure drills, such as picking up our gear and 'grounding it,' and the supervisor would repeat the exercises until all six hundred recruits were in perfect unison. Improper behavior of any kind resulted in the loss of a 'demerit card,' which we personalized and were required to carry at all times. Three demerit cards equaled a 'CD,' or a 'Command Discipline,'

35

placed in your personnel file. Multiple CDs could lead to a hearing, and possible termination.

However, it wasn't about losing days off, or even the threat of getting fired. There were many blistering summer afternoons on that muster deck when I stood at some variation of attention, staring silently at the head in front of me, sweating from the intense heat, muscles aching from not being able to fidget, annoying itches going unscratched. Still, I didn't move, and neither did anyone else.

They had given each of us three yellow pieces of paper and told us to write our names on them. It was my intention to keep all three pieces, to show to my future children someday, if they should ever decide to follow in my footsteps. I didn't want to embarrass myself or my company, or the silly gray costume that I was required to wear.

It became more than just about a paycheck, a pension plan, or any status they might eventually give me.

It was about pride.

***

During our days at the building, the Academy felt a lot like high school.

We had three classroom subjects - Law, Social Science, and Police Science. We also had a daily gym period, and a meal hour. In addition, there were also many interesting field trips. We had firearms training in the Bronx at a place called Rodman's Neck, a private outdoor firing range. We drove police cars over orange construction cones at Floyd Bennett Field, a federal reserve that rented space to the NYPD for driving drills. We visited the medical examiner's office to smell death and formaldehyde, we sat in courtrooms to witness hearings and arraignments, we entered fake apartments to get "shot" at by actors with fake hidden guns. It was a proverbial roller coaster ride that would end with three milestones: Gun & Shield Day, the tour during which we would finally be trusted to take home our most dangerous piece of equipment; FTU, a one-month field training assignment to a random precinct; Lastly, the graduation ceremony at Madison Square Garden.

Regarding our firearms, my particular company was required to choose our pistols in our first week at the Academy. As a group, we were taken down into the basement of the building, next to an indoor shooting range. One at a time, we were introduced to both the Glock 17 and the Smith & Wesson 5946, the only authorized choices in 1997, both with the firing pins taken out. Even fully loaded, they were powerless.

I remember standing at the table, with both guns and a veteran standing beside me. He wore a khaki-colored version of the NYPD uniform, indicating his assignment to the Firearms Division. He told me to pick them up, one at a time, and point them at an imaginary target, to see which one I liked better. We were told that our choice would be permanent, for the rest of our police careers.

At the time, that seemed stupid to me. Secretly, I wished that I could fire a few rounds out of each, to have some sort of frame of reference, something to compare. I would find out later that my worries were irrelevant, that a gun is just that - a gun. You aim and pull the trigger. If respected properly, it is a harmless piece of metal. But in the hands of someone irresponsible or malicious, they are all equally deadly. On a hunch, I picked the Smith.

It's hard to explain what it feels like to fire a gun for the first time.

I remember my entire company standing, side-by-side, out on an enclosed grassy field a few months later, our toes on a line painted across a strip of concrete. Dozens of brass shell casings littered the ground all around us, from previous groups that tried in vain to completely clear away their collective mess. We wore headsets to protect our hearing, and plastic goggles for our eyes. Our firearms rested quietly at our sides, the leather from our virgin duty belts not yet broken in. For most of the day at Rodman's Neck, I carried my strange new friend on my hip, instructed to ignore it under penalty of termination. And at the end of the tour, all the guns were rounded up by khaki cops and thrown into a locked trailer until our next training session.

But on that line, under strict supervision, they did let us experiment.

Twenty-eight men and women, sweating under the blaring sun through polyester shirts and distracted by the extra weight of that duty rig fastened around our waists, all waiting anxiously to pull the trigger. Honestly, I was curious and excited and afraid, all at once. Covering a paper target, my arms began to ache from holding the heavy Smith with arms extended. I was wondering if the Glock recruits were experiencing the same issue, when suddenly, it happened.

BzzzzzZZZzzz.

The entire area exploded with the sound of firecrackers, muffled by ear protection, but still alarming. My peripheral vision was mostly blocked by my goggles, but that didn't prevent me from seeing two spent brass shell casings fly over from the right, ejected from the gun of the recruit alongside me. When I pulled my own trigger, the cold, quiet steel erupted in my hands. I couldn't believe how loud it was.

Next, we were all told to holster and proceed downhill, to see our targets up close. I was happy with this, because I needed a minute to dwell on the experience. Plus, I didn't see my target change. Yes, I saw the smoke and muzzle flash, and the pistol jumping in my hand, but my paper looked unchanged. I thought maybe I had missed my board altogether. I walked downfield with the rest of my company, to investigate.

Sure enough, they were there. Two tiny holes, both in the shoulder of the vague human drawing.

Already, recruits in 97-20 were becoming competitive with this new game, comparing and evaluating. Some had hit the center of the gray mass, a perfect shot. Others had missed the silhouette and the paper altogether, finding either a clean sheet or three holes in the target next door. Honestly, it was an interesting skill, placing the holes exactly where you wanted them to go. I liked it, and much later it would become one of my hobbies. Sometimes, while off-duty, I would go to a private range, buy a cheap box of ammo and fire away. It was a good stress release, and I became good at it. However, lack of money and time got in the way, and I eventually had to stop my sessions - for other reasons.

Anyway, back at the Academy building, we had a daily gym period. Each session would start off with a run, led by an instructor, each of us wearing white cotton t-shirts with our name and company number boldly printed on the front. There was always an intense pressure not to drop out of the run, from the administration as well as from within the company. It began as a half-mile, the distance steadily increasing as the summer days crawled along beside us. I wasn't the best runner in the world, but I never dropped out.

After the run, we would also endure basic calisthenics. The exercise wasn't that rigorous, but it was a very humid summer in '97, and the gymnasium had no air conditioning. By the time our push-ups and sit-ups were finally done, we each sat in a pond of our own sweat, dreaming of cool shower water falling on us. Sometimes, anonymous administrators and bosses would evaluate us from the second-floor balcony, probably checking to see who would give up and who wouldn't, scribbling notes and checking off boxes in their mystery binders and notebooks.

On a random day, I remember seeing a group of unfamiliar men above, watching our gym block with interest. They all sported brown uniforms and stood with a soldier's posture, each wearing a sky blue beret. At the time, I had no idea which organization they represented -

40

and I still don't - but it was obvious that they were from some military or law enforcement agency, curious about the NYPD's training methods. Obviously, I wasn't the only one that noticed, as our gym instructor intentionally picked up the pace. In unison, we all did jumping jacks like madmen underneath a large banner that read:

"YOU ARE A MEMBER OF

NEW YORK'S FINEST!"

With my heart racing and my lungs about to explode, I never wanted to believe those words more than I did that day, while under the watchful eyes of those who had come to see what the most renowned police department in the world had to offer.

For the record, I never gave up.

Not on that day, or any other.

***

NYPD Officer Anthony Sanchez worked midnight patrol in the 13th precinct in Manhattan, the entrance to his station house on the opposite side of the same block as the Academy building. He was a ten-year veteran with a wife

41

and a house on Long Island, where I was told he would spend afternoons caring for his seven-year old son before returning to work in the evenings.

The story of his murder was on every TV screen and radio station that morning in May 1997 as I hauled my heavy bag through quiet streets, that Sanchez and his partner responded to a '10-30' call — the radio code for a robbery in progress - in a luxury co-op penthouse during the overnight, that he had been shot by a man who had tried to rob his own father. With no prior criminal record, the injured son was later found cowering in the basement of that Chelsea building with superficial bullet wounds to his chest and forearm. Tragically, Sanchez was not so lucky, as he was transported to a nearby ER by frantic police officers in the back of a patrol car, but to no avail.

Our Academy assignment two days later was to find a small town in Long Island called West Babylon, being one of the few companies chosen at random to attend his funeral. My little morning group drove by carpool - myself, John D'Angelo, and two other recruits - and parked at the end of a dusty rural road that led to an isolated church built on an incline, surrounded by open grass fields.

As I walked the winding dirt trail bordered by haphazard wire fences, I was truly stunned.

They had come from everywhere.

Not just police officers, but firemen, sanitation workers, federal agents, even military personnel from every branch, all dressed in formal gear and walking the road along with us — making small talk, parking their personal cars, looking for convenience stores to buy food or cigarettes — all of them taking time out of their busy schedules to pay respects to a fallen officer that they never met, and never would.

The official tally was more than ten thousand. I remember four jet aircraft in diamond formation breaking the sound barrier directly above us. Our distant position alongside the road did not allow us a view of the church, but we were close enough to hear the singing of bagpipes. We raised our right hands in salute as dark vehicles crept past us and disappeared up the hill. We didn't see the pallbearers or hear the tributes from the mayor and the police commissioner, which surely had little significance to Elizabeth, his widowed wife, or John, his young son. Police brass and others would call him a hero many times that day, but that would do little to ease the pain of his partner, his squad, or his precinct.

Anthony Sanchez.

The photograph that had been splashed across the front pages of the New York newspapers was from his identification card, very similar to a mugshot. He didn't look Spanish, with pale skin and light brown buzzcut. Like me, he looked like a stereotypical white boy with a Latin last name who had taken a city test and passed.

I looked around me, at all the other people that routinely walked in his shoes, every night.

Standing there, I imagined that one day I would raise my right hand, this time at my graduation ceremony, and be honored to walk along with the rest. I'd find the right

43

girl, get married, buy a dream house of my own, maybe pop out a kid or two. And then one night, ten years later, my partner and I would get a routine call that would return me to that same dusty road where I stood, either in tears or in a casket.

In that moment, I knew I was wrong.

They *all* knew him, every morning they looked in a mirror. They all wore a uniform, carried a shield, swore an oath, performed a duty.

They were all heroes, every last one of them, and on that day they had congregated to say goodbye to one of their own.

Since that day, I understood.

***

One of the proudest moments in any cop's career is the day they are given their gun and shield.

In the NYPD, it usually happens towards the end of the Academy, as recruits begin their one month of field training at a random precinct. Until that day, even though I was already on the city payroll as a police officer, I still felt like a civilian being paid to go to school.

It was a night tour in September. The six hundred day tour cops had already left the building with their new

44

toys, probably either scared silly or doing cartwheels, and now it was our turn. It was an empty day with no other agenda, just a buzz of electricity hanging in the air. I could taste it on my tongue as they filed us into the third-floor auditorium to do nothing, just sit and wait. Academy brass took turns pronouncing us the chosen ones, ready for the challenge. My chest felt like it might explode from anticipation.

When the time arrived, we were told to form a single line in alphabetical order. I was last in line. As we were about to head for the stairwell, our instructor, a young Irish cop who was on the verge of promotion and counting down the days himself, pulled me aside.

"You have to wait here, to guard the gear," he told me.

The black bags.

Twenty-seven total, lining the walls. They held nothing valuable, and no one would think of touching them.

However, I was given an order, so I followed it.

Finally, the company sergeant returned to the room and I headed downstairs, three steps at a time. I passed classmates who were already returning, a shiny piece of metal pinned to their shirts, wide-eyed like they had just seen Santa Claus. At the bottom of the stairwell was a dimly lit corridor, nearly deserted. Far ahead was the back of a gray shirt, a dead giveaway. I got on the back of the line, realizing that I was about to enter the indoor firing range, a place that we had never been allowed to go before.

45

As I waited and moved forward a few inches at a time, an old man who had once stood on that line himself rambled about safety and responsibility and where to find the best deals on ammo.

Finally, they positioned me inside a shooting stall, staring down at a paper target. They asked me my surname, and dropped a plastic box on the ledge in front of me. It was the same box that I had opened and closed several times before, at Rodman's Neck. We were given explicit instructions. Open the box, finger off the trigger, holster the gun, and then forget it exists. We had been told several versions of a story about a recruit that had shot a hole through a bathroom stall fifteen minutes after getting his firearm, after which he was promptly instructed to give it back and find another job.

That might have been just an elaborate scare tactic, but it worked on me.

After that, there was another small room, empty except for a single instructor, sitting at a desk.

"What's your number?" he asked.

"Two-five-five-seven-five," I responded, memorized from my ID card.

Many times, I wondered if someone had worn those numbers before me, about the brave or funny stories that might be attached to them. Regardless, I hoped that they would bring me good luck, and that I would bestow upon them a notable history in return.

46

In the end, I absolutely would - but not in the way that I had hoped.

The teacher looked down and found what he was looking for, cavalierly flipping a tissue paper-covered shield in my direction. I caught it with both hands against my stomach, like a kid would catch a football. I expected it to feel like a rock, but it was absurdly light. I ripped off the paper and held it in my palm, reading the numbers, again and again.

"Good luck," he told me, as I stumbled off down the corridor in a daze, still staring.

I just couldn't take my eyes off it.

It was the most amazing thing.

The City of New York had decided to put their trust in me, to carry out the laws of the state.

They had just given me the authority to take a person's freedom away in the pursuit of justice.

As a last resort, they had granted me the power over life and death, at the flick of a finger.

The embodiment of all that rested very plainly in my possession, in a small piece of metal with a five-digit number.

My number.

That light piece of tin, at that moment, became me.

***

It was the "collar" from Hell.

It was during my field training at Manhattan North, and it was my formal introduction to both the arrest process and Murphy's Law.

The aforementioned arrest was during a sweep of unlicensed general vendors. The commanding officer at the North decided that during one day a week the trainees would rid themselves of the gray uniform, dress up in civilian clothing and hunt merchants walking the streets selling wares without the proper paperwork.

This was considered a big deal at the 18th Precinct, as peddlers would frequently undercut legit businesses, which would cause store owners to scream bloody murder at community board meetings about their high rents and their inability to compete with these walking salesmen. Thus, on occasion, with a portable radio hidden away in an inside pocket, we would wander the streets. In our travels, if a vendor would open his briefcase to show off fake Rolex watches and such, we then had the probable cause needed for an arrest.

One night, while strolling down Seventh Avenue looking for a UGV collar and getting impatient, I noticed something else that was also illegal, so I took the initiative.

Of course, I had no idea that I was about to crash into a wall of technological and procedural failures that would make me feel just as much like a prisoner as the accused.

But again, I'm getting ahead of myself.

About a week earlier, I was involved in a bicycle summonsing detail, another glorious Manhattan condition. According to our training sergeant, bicycles are subject to the same laws that regulate motor vehicles, which basically means that anything that a cop can give a car a ticket for - like going the wrong way down a one-way street, or even riding on the sidewalk - they can also give to a bicycle.

One day during one of those revenue binges, I noticed a bicyclist riding on the sidewalk right next to me.

Bingo. I had nine tickets already, and the target number for the day was ten.

I motioned for him to stop and get off the bike, which he did.

"What did I do?" he asked innocently. He was a black male in his twenties, well over six feet tall. He wore a nylon sack with a chest strap, the universal badge of the working bike messenger.

"You were riding on the sidewalk, sir," I told him. "You're not allowed to do that."

"No, I wasn't," he said in a cool, even voice.

"In any event, I'm going to need to see some I.D.," I responded. There was no need to argue. I would get his driver's license, write the summons, and he could tell the judge his version of the story. Hopefully, he could concoct a convincing argument and pay a reduced fine.

Well, Mr. Ten's response was short, and to the point.

"No."

"Excuse me?"

"I don't have to give you my license," he answered, still calm and respectful. "I didn't do anything wrong."

"First of all, yes you did," I answered, slowly descending into a debate. "And I'm asking you to show me some identification."

"I don't want to."

At that point, I honestly didn't know what to do. *Didn't he see the uniform that I was wearing?* Here I was, in the uniform of a New York City police officer. Growing up in the city myself, I would never have imagined refusing a request from a cop. *How could this be happening?*

"I'm going to ask you one more time," I said to him, trying to be as respectful as possible. "I need to see your I.D."

50

"I don't have to give you my I.D."

Did he? All of a sudden, I was thrown into a sea of doubt. What did I have the power to do? I was new at this, and I didn't want to get into trouble. *Could I force him? Could I go into his pockets? Was it even worth it?*

I hesitated as my partner for the day, a female recruit from Long Island who supposedly had gone to school with music superstar Mariah Carey, crossed the street to join me.

She heard my side of the story, and took a different approach.

"Listen to me," she said sharply, like she was trying to cut him with her words. Suddenly, I realized that the bicyclist was not six feet tall. My partner was five-foot-four, and their eyes were on the same level, her nose almost touching his face. "If you don't stop wasting our time, I'm gonna lock your ass up and throw away the fucking key. You got that?"

With that, he calmly reached into his back pocket and got his license, giving it to her without hesitation.

I was totally amazed. Quickly, I wrote the ticket, and he was off without another word.

Later on at the station house, still baffled, I cornered the training sergeant.

"A summons is in lieu of arrest," he told me, a heavy guy that, by the look of his sloppy uniform, should have been working in a different borough. "Do you know what that means?"

"Not really."

"It's a courtesy," he answered, sitting at a desk and counting our tickets for the day. "You're trusting him to show up and see the judge in thirty days. However, anything that you can write that summons for, you can also lock him up."

"What if someone refuses to give you identification?"

"Of course," he answered, nonchalantly.

I was still confused. Obviously, he saw it on my face.

"Look... You don't know this guy from Adam," he continued, as if I were a six-year-old that should know by now not to touch the wall socket. "He could've just fled the scene of a crime in which he killed three people. If he refuses to give you identification, you treat him like he is until he proves otherwise. You give him *one* chance, ask him nicely. If he refuses, then you throw him on a wall, put handcuffs on him, and drag him back to the precinct. Let him sit in a cell while you get yourself coffee and a Slim Jim."

"But what if he makes a complaint?" I asked.

The Academy had made us terrified of CCRBs, the acronym for the Civilian Complaint Review Board, the legislative body that handed out complaints against cops.

"So?" he responded, smiling through years of experience. "Criminals will *always* make complaints. Next to breaking the law, it's their favorite pastime. But on the street, YOU are the boss. Your goal is to do your job correctly and get home safe. Never be afraid to take action. If you hesitate, you might get hurt someday."

Those words of wisdom were rattling around in my head as I walked the streets in blue jeans a week later, my shield hanging from a beaded chain on my neck but concealed under a t-shirt. My partner for the night, an Asian kid who had worked for IBM previously but was much happier in the Academy, was window-shopping on the opposite side of the street, keeping in step with me, occasionally making eye contact. Our job that night was to walk and be patient, waiting for a UGV to cross our paths.

Obviously, I was still annoyed with myself. I had been intimidated, and I was determined to not let that happen again. Unfortunately, after an hour walking on Seventh Avenue, not a single vendor said hello.

It was in this aggressive state of mind that I finally found my very first collar.

I arrested a homeless person who was ballroom dancing with an invisible partner, bumping into people and begging for loose change.

Now, nine out of ten cops probably would've just kept walking. But of course, I had a personal vendetta on the brain. Dancing in public isn't against the law, nor is begging for change, especially if you're doing it quietly at the base of a building. However, obstructing pedestrian traffic is a rarely-used subdivision of Disorderly Conduct, a violation punishable by a summons, or a trip through the system.

A light went off in my head, and I pounced.

Within seconds, he was facing the wall with my handcuffs around his wrists. With the thought of open sores and diseases creeping into my subconscious, a ticket seemed like the best choice, until I found a glass tube filled with drug residue in his back pocket.

Instantly upgraded to a misdemeanor - criminal possession of a controlled substance - I no longer had that option. He was now a keeper, which made me happy.

However, my glee would be only temporary.

In the Academy, I had been given a neat list of steps regarding the arrest process. Certain paperwork had to be filled out, in a particular order, all with the prisoner in tow. But life is not as simple as a list.

Every borough has a slightly different spin, each precinct with their own unique way of processing an arrest, catering to the layout of the individual command and its supervisors. Sometimes just finding the right room that holds the paperwork is a daunting task. That shouldn't have been a problem, since I couldn't have been expected to know what I was doing.

I needed assistance, someone to hold my hand and guide me through the process.

No such luck.

So, I made the arrest at about ten-thirty PM, with my tour ending at 2335 hours military time, or eleven thirty-five. I knew that I would be getting some overtime, as an average arrest normally takes about three hours, from start to finish.

However, by the time a police vehicle picked me and my human cargo up, it was a quarter to eleven. The disgusted look on the face of the lieutenant at the desk, wanting to know why I had brought "trash" into her house, occurred at eleven on the dot. By the time I searched the prisoner, took off the handcuffs and placed him in the holding cell, it was already sign out time. The training officer assigned to my group from the Academy had no clue where the paperwork was located either, so he was no help. Besides, he conveniently snuck away and went home.

Thus, I was stuck with this human being as my responsibility, with only a vague idea of what to do with him.

Now, had I been permanently assigned to 18th Precinct, the nice Lieu at the desk would have been responsible for my overtime and would have immediately assigned someone to make sure that I wasn't milking it. But as property of the Police Academy, the school would get the bill for my overtime, not the North.

I could have the entire cow, as far as she was concerned.

Eventually, I got my hands on most of the paperwork. Luckily, I wasn't alone in my confusion, as another Academy cop was also in the house on overtime, processing a UGV collar. His name was Mark, a quiet Irish kid, and he would become my shadow for the next sixteen hours. Normally, it might take a veteran an hour or two to finish the written stuff. Putting our heads together, we didn't finish until two AM.

Next, we needed to send the details via computer to Albany. Every cop is given an access code when they get to their permanent commands, but not in FTU. Thankfully, a rookie at the desk gave us his code when the Lieu was distracted, and we proceeded to hack and slash our way through an unforgiving program that wasn't at all pleased with our civilian terminology. Standing on Seventh Avenue, I remembered being happy. Overtime meant time-and-a-half, money added to my paycheck. But now it was already three AM, with no end in sight. Ironically, while I was drowning in fatigue and uncertainty, my prisoner stretched out on the floor of the holding cell, fast asleep. *Who is the prisoner here? Him or me?*

Next was a machine called LiveScan, which neither Mark nor I had ever seen before.

At a glance, it looked like an ATM. After closer inspection, we realized that it was a new computerized fingerprinting device. Our task seemed simple: wake up our perps, drag them out of the cell to stand next to the LiveScan, to roll each fingertip onto a glass countertop. Mark went first and finished quickly, which seemed to be a good sign. When he was done, a midnight cop asked to cut the line, so I waited.

When it was my turn, the machine decided to take an extended coffee break, to "recalibrate."

Next, I was told by telephone that "Albany was down," which meant that I had to wait some more.

At five AM, the Lieu wanted to know why the hell my perp was still in her house and not at Central Booking, which is a big holding cell for the entire borough. Without a coherent answer, she told me to forget LiveScan and use old-fashioned ink cards. In the meantime, Mark had been trying to fax his paperwork to the District Attorney's office, but of the two functioning fax machines in the entire building, one was acting belligerent and the other was locked upstairs in a detective's office.

After figuring that out, despite being frustrated and exhausted, I was rapidly cheering up. After a fifteen-hour tour, the end seemed near. Wearing corrective lenses, my vision was so dry and blurry at that point that I was almost better off without them. However, I'd be able to rip them off soon and finally get to bed.

Or so I thought.

Taking a deep sigh of relief, we both approached the desk with our happy news. I had my pen in my hand, ready to sign the roll call and sprint upstairs to my locker. That was when the Lieutenant held out a set of car keys, nonchalantly.

"Take Van five-two-eight-one. Does either one of you know how to get to Manhattan Central Booking?" she asked. Of course, since we were guests at the precinct, it hadn't occurred to me that we might be asked to transport the prisoners ourselves.

"I do," Mark said, and she threw the keys at him.

"Don't forget to report back here at eight AM... for a full tour," she told us, matter-of-factly. "In uniform."

Standing there, it took a moment for process this. I had already worked a full five-day workweek. Tomorrow would be my sixth day in a row. Besides, it was already six AM. Obviously, there would be no time to go home or to get any sleep, and a full tour starting in two hours would finish at five PM, for a grand total of *twenty-six hours straight*, the equivalent of working three tours in a row.

"You've got to be *fucking* kidding me," I told myself.

Unfortunately, I also said it out loud.

"Absolutely not, officer," she said, with an annoyed look on her face. I'm sure that she wasn't used to open defiance, especially from Academy brats. "You are required to meet with the lawyer to draw up the official charges against your prisoner... So get your ass moving to Central Booking."

Mark bolted for the holding cell, and I stumbled sluggishly after him. When my partner for the night was out of earshot, she called me back over to the desk.

"I've been in your shoes a dozen times," she told me. The Lieutenant was probably an Italian woman in her forties, with short dark hair. In other circumstances, she might have been attractive, but in that moment, her presence was too distracting. "*You* chose this life. No one else. Sometimes, you don't go home. That's just the way it is."

I remember being too tired to respond, and besides, there was nothing to say.

She was right.

Before she sent me on my way, she made a statement that I would believe wholeheartedly and repeat several times in my very short career.

"This is not a job. This is a lifestyle."

And so it was.

***

Maria.

I met her off-duty, late one night.

It was a weekly routine: local bar to drink and play pool with a few civilian friends, then fill up on greasy food at a diner before crawling into bed. One particular evening, as we chatted about the local girls who paid very little attention to us, two women - a brunette and a blonde - entered the restaurant and made their way past our table to an adjacent booth. I remember very little about the brunette, as she would fade from my memory as the complicated story of Maria and I was about to begin.

She was very beautiful. Deep brown eyes and soft features surrounded by golden hair. That night, she wore a dressy blue blouse and a mid-length black skirt which showcased an athletic figure. My goal was to make eye contact, perhaps start a conversation, and just hope for the best.

My prayers were quickly answered. She fired the first flare in our direction, requesting a light for her unlit cigarette. Remember, this was the late 1990's when indoor smoking at diners was still permitted. My friend Rob, in possession of a Zippo, did the honors. I proceeded to turn my chair to face her directly, and the small talk began.

"What did you ladies do tonight?" I asked, staring only at her.

"Sang Karaoke," she responded politely, referring to the sing-along frenzy first made popular in Japan. As an attraction, local bar owners would host 'Karaoke Nights,' where patrons would sing along with the instrumentals of a popular song, while watching a TV screen that featured the lyrics.

60

"Have you ever done it?" she asked me.

"What exactly are you referring to, my dear?" I responded, trying to be cute.

"Karaoke," she answered, smiling briefly.

"Of course," I said. "Alone in the car, in the shower..."

"You should try it in front of people. It's fun."

"Not my thing. But I would try it if you'd join me. For moral support, of course."

A close-mouthed smile, but then it disappeared. "Maybe."

Unfortunately, our food was done just as theirs was being served. We would walk out, and surely I would never see her again. I had no pen to write down my telephone number, and I didn't want to ask for hers and put her on the spot. I had marked it up to poor timing, and was content to just go home.

That was when Rob reached into his front pocket to retrieve a stack of folded money. In the center was a business card. On the reverse side of that card was my beeper number, in my own handwriting. Luckily, I had just given him that card, to beep me when he finished work. Wordlessly, he placed the card on the table and slid it across to me.

When we left, I thanked her for the chat, and placed the card on her table.

61

Two hours later, my pager vibrated in my pocket.

Two hours after that, I found myself in bed with her.

Maria was light-years ahead of me. I was twenty-five and single, never married, no kids, starting a new career and secretly looking to start a family of my own. She, on the other hand, was twenty-nine, already married but separated, and in the process of a messy divorce involving four kids. Of course, I was wary of her situation, so I resolved to play it safe.

I made a vow to myself not to get trapped, and if things went bad, I would say goodbye.

Unfortunately, that was a promise my heart couldn't keep.

Also, my relationship with Maria would directly impact my job, and the end of this story.

But I'm not ready to talk about that yet.

**

I remember not being able to sleep, as if it was Christmas morning.

In many ways, it was.

It was still dark out when the alarm clock sang an annoying, familiar tune. Excited, I got up quickly, even though I had given myself plenty of time. The house that I shared with my father, mother and younger sister was silent, as they continued to sleep peacefully. They had all arranged to take off from work and planned to join me later, but there was no reason for them to be awake yet.

However, like twelve hundred other happy people that morning, I was required to arrive early, to help prepare.

Like other mornings, I found my car and sped over to D'Angelo's house to pick him up. We were long since in the habit of driving all the way down to the Academy building, taking turns paying for a private lot. However, the Academy was not our destination that morning, as we parked at the local train station and endured the subway one last time with nostalgic smiles. I remember watching as the train descended under the belly of the Bronx and thinking about my field training at Manhattan North. As the FTU days wound down, I realized that I wanted to stay there. I made two more arrests before my month was up — this time UGVs - and was learning how to shorten the process. Going back to that sloppy training sergeant, I asked if there was any way that a recruit could defect to his command. He said no with a grin. There are other great places to work, he told me.

In retrospect, he was absolutely right.

Our stop was Penn Station - the entrance located on Seventh Avenue between 31st and 33rd Streets in downtown Manhattan. Resting directly above us was the fabled Madison Square Garden, an arena rich with history and fanfare, the home of two professional sports franchises, the Knicks and the Rangers. In addition to many other events, the New York City Police Department would rent the place on occasion to hold a private celebration of its own. Finally, it was graduation day, a grand event that marked the end of our hard work, and the beginning of what we all hoped would be successful and storied careers.

In a flash, I found myself marching onto the Garden floor, single file toward a folding chair as the applause of thousands filled my eardrums. With my eyes trained on the head in front of me, I saw very little of the crowd, or the stage for that matter, with high-ranking officials and politicians speaking highly of us and patting themselves on the back for their part in our creation. We all stood at attention, and at the command of the master of ceremonies, our gloved right hands surged up in military salute, like hundreds of white doves emerging beneath a vast material ocean of midnight blue. Again the crowd erupted, and their cheers floated down as a reward for our efforts. Shortly after, we were commanded to sit again as one solid entity, heads locked forward and our hands firmly on our knees, as all the praises and predictions continued.

Sitting still, there was nothing to do but think.

That blue application paper, waiting on the coffee table in my mind's eye.

The chill of York College, the humidity and stink of the Academy gym block, the smell of burnt gunpowder at Rodman's Neck.

The classrooms, the field excursions, all the months of obstacles moved aside. They were all there, on a large projection screen in my head.

Like an out-of-body experience, I watched the past lead into the present, as the graduates around me tossed our eight-point caps high into the air, symbolic of our grand achievement.

But I also saw my future, both near and far.

I watched myself meet with my family after the ceremony, eat a celebratory dinner, toast to a bright future ahead.

A brick and mortar building on the corner of 181st Street and Ryer Avenue in the Bronx would become my home, and I would walk my first foot post, answer radio runs in a sector car, and occasionally make difficult decisions.

I saw myself learning that being a police officer is often a front-row seat to life, as I charged into situations that people instinctively run away from, often taking my own safety for granted. I would discover that this new lifestyle was both the best and the worst job in the world, sometimes both in the same tour.

Surprisingly, I also saw myself reach top pay after five years, sacrifice my Saturdays to take promotional exams, to wear the white shirt of a Lieutenant or a Captain. After my twenty years of honorable service, I could see myself using my experience in law enforcement as a gateway into the private sector, maybe a security manager for a Fortune 500 company.

After that, a run at local politics, as a state senator or assemblyman.

Five and Twenty.

It was one hell of a movie.

And I saw it all very clearly, time standing still on the Garden floor, as if it had already happened.

With supreme confidence, I believed that life could only be fair, that hardworking people always get what they deserve, and that nothing on earth - short of a gunman's bullet - could stop me.

Nothing.

FIVE

March 16, 1999.

The Captain's Office.

First of all, the following must be said.

At some point in your reading of this book, you may decide, due to my civilian background or my associations with certain individuals, or even from my conduct in uniform, that I didn't deserve to be a police officer.

And that's fine.

I'm fully aware that some of my behavior - both on and off-duty - was questionable, even hypocritical. Some of the things in the pages ahead may even strengthen such convictions.

Again, I am by no means a saint, nor do I pretend to be one. You are free to pass judgment, and I simply thank you for taking the time to read this far.

Having said that, these are the facts.

I did not use cocaine.

Not ever.

Not before I took the initial written exam at Roosevelt High School.

Not during my time as a cop.

And never in the twenty-plus years since.

However, according to the NYPD, I absolutely did.

And under the zero-tolerance rules of the New York City Police Department, that was enough to end my career.

That fact will never change, and like it or not, it has become a part of my personal legacy.

Regardless, none of that had dawned on me yet as I sat in my private car on the side of the road with that sergeant from Internal Affairs. I understood their purpose, but nothing about their visit made the slightest amount of sense, and it never will.

More than ever, I needed time to recover, to think things through.

Unfortunately for me, it wasn't necessary for them to afford me that courtesy.

"You do have options," the sergeant told me. His speech seemed prepared. "You tested positive for cocaine in two of your hair samples. You opted for the department to take a third sample, which is currently locked away at the

Medical Division in police custody. At your own expense, you can choose to have that third sample tested. However, since the *first* sample has been tested and it came back positive, and then the second sample *also* came back positive, what's the chance that the third will be any different?"

It was a rhetorical question, but I couldn't help myself.

"But I didn't do it."

My mind was swirling, and I was fighting with my emotions. I was trying to keep quiet, to stay under control and make a good impression, not realizing until later that the sergeant was just doing his job and probably didn't care either way. He continued.

"In any event, if you choose to test that third sample, you will be suspended without pay, effective immediately. You will have a thirty-day appeal period, after which you will most likely be terminated."

"Will there be a trial?" I asked.

"No," he said, but immediately offered an explanation. "Unfortunately, you are not entitled to a department trial since you are technically not off probation. It was your end-of-probation exam when they took your hair."

They had told us that, back in the Academy. It would be our final step.

They would take hair twice: Once during the application process, and then again at the two-year mark.

My hair came back negative in 1997.

Then, on February 26, 1999, I reported at the beginning of my regularly scheduled tour to Lefrak City, knowing exactly why I was there, to allow a cop to shave clumps of hair from my chest.

That night, the details of February 26th were still fresh in my mind. Coincidentally, Maria had been involved in a minor car accident and had called my cell phone, while I was waiting in line. I called 911 on her behalf as I inched forward, and then she called back to tell me that a police report was being taken, that everything was fine, and that she loved me. Afterwards, I told jokes as a cop in latex gloves dropped my shavings into three anonymously-marked, number-coordinated bags — two of them in plastic, the third optional one in paper - and then I headed off to Bronx traffic court to testify regarding a ticket that I had written on patrol.

Besides already knowing the time frame of my end-of-probation medical exam, which would hover around my two-year anniversary, I also knew the exact date of the trip, having been notified almost three weeks in advance.

None of it made any sense, I thought to myself. *I knew the test was coming. Why would I voluntarily give hair if I knew I had drugs in my system?*

"There is another option," the sergeant said, interrupting the intense conversation that I was having with myself. "We could take a trip downtown, to our office. We could sit down, discuss things. Maybe we can find a way to send you to work tomorrow."

"What do you mean?" I asked, still hopeful.

"Maybe you might be able to tell us something... helpful? Something about the people that you work with. Things... happen. You help us, and maybe we can help you."

Obviously, he was looking for corruption, names of dirty cops who might have crossed my path.

To the best of my knowledge, I had only worked with honorable people. Even in my sadness, I could see what was happening. In his mind, he had a cokehead at his disposal, to manipulate and exploit. I felt like my head was about to explode. I knew nothing, and I told him so.

Staring hopelessness in the face, I politely asked if I could go home.

Unwilling to give up on me just yet, he called the lieutenant over the radio. The Lieu again crouched near my open car window, and the sergeant advised him of my decision. He then went back to his squad car for a few minutes, and I could see him talking on a cell phone through the back windshield, despite the dark tint. Then, he returned.

"The Captain would appreciate it if you would come to the office," he told me, with humility in his voice. "You are not obligated. He would just like an opportunity to speak to you."

Honestly, there was nothing left to say. It had all been explained quite well, and I couldn't handle much more. Feeling defeated, I wanted nothing more than to crawl into bed and hide forever.

But in my heart, I was still a police officer.

True, I wasn't obligated to go anywhere. But if a Captain wanted to see me, I went.

The sergeant drove, as I sat in the passenger seat of my own car. Actually, it seemed fitting since I no longer felt in control of my destiny. Unable to focus, I paid very little attention to the landmarks or street signs. Soon, we entered a tall building, somewhere in Manhattan. The only thing I vividly remember was a bright circle of yellow light, the button in the elevator that said we were headed to the sixteenth floor.

Once inside his office, the Captain appeared exactly as I had imagined him.

About six feet tall, he was a Caucasian in his fifties with a heavy mustache and thinning hair. He wore a relaxed business outfit - beige shirt, unbuttoned at the neck, khaki slacks and light brown loafers. He seemed extremely familiar, and then it hit me: I had seen the Captain on that imaginary screen in my head on graduation day. He was exactly what I wanted to be.

As a result, I was overcome with the desire to convince him that I had been wrongfully accused.

I think it would have been easier to ask an atheist to believe in God.

"Look," he said to me at one point. "*I* know that you did it. *You* know that you did it. I'm not asking for a confession. I don't have a checklist, where I keep a record of how many guys crack under the pressure. I just want to give you your gun and shield back, and send you to work tomorrow."

Obviously, he only wanted dirt.

"I have no information for you. If I did, you would have already been notified," I told him, noticing a revolver strapped to his ankle as he crossed his legs. At home, I owned a similar gun, a snub-nose blue steel Smith & Wesson .38 caliber that was almost an antique, the previous owner a Vietnam War veteran. It was my third and final purchase.

"But that's not what's important, sir," I said, respectfully. "I did *not* use cocaine. There's been a mistake."

"These are the facts," he responded, a grin on his face. "If you took your bare hand and stuck it into a pillowcase filled with cocaine, your hair test would register

73

about two or three nanograms, due to exposure through the pores of your skin. Because of this, you are allowed to register up to five nanograms, to account for incidental contact. Your hair samples came back at fourteen-point-one, and fourteen-point-nine, which means that within the last six months, you did coke at least once."

"Then it cannot be my hair, or the lab fucked up," I said, defiantly.

"Look... the company that tests the hair has the entire NYPD account, which means it has the responsibility of testing *thousands* of cops. This is how it works: They test the first sample. If it comes back under five nanograms, they throw all of your stuff away - everything - and they go on to the next person. But if it's above five, they give your second sample to a different lab technician, who tests it. When that second sample *also* pops positive, they send us the bad news. Now, it's time for me to ask you a question," he said, leaning forward in his seat. There was nothing separating us as we sat on cheap folding chairs, facing each other in an empty room with bay windows that overlooked a dark city and its many flickering lights. "Do you think that the drug company wants to risk not only its reputation, but a multi-million dollar account with the NYPD and open themselves up to a lawsuit? If there was *anything* shaky with either one of your samples - a tainted batch, or confusion over who the hair actually belonged to - it would be easy enough for them to just toss out your hair and send back a negative result."

Even from my perspective, it made sense.

74

I knew that if I were sitting in his chair, as I desperately wanted to be, I wouldn't have believed a single word that came out of my mouth.

Also, I realized that even if he did buy my story, he probably had no control over the situation. His computer told him that I was positive. He was simply acting on that information, doing his job the way I would have if the roles were reversed.

On another level that I was trying very hard to ignore, I honestly believed that there was no way that I would be allowed to go back to work the next day. It was all just an elaborate ploy, to get dirt on other corrupt cops.

But none of that changed the truth.

Given the choice, I would rather have died that night than cause a visit to that office.

Even if I had been stupid enough to snort a line of coke right before the dole test, I was smart enough to walk away.

After three hours of back and forth, a new option was suddenly laid on the table. I was told that I would be allowed to resign.

To this day, I am not sure why. He did mention my family, that his minions had paid them an afternoon visit. My younger sister had just been married, and she and my mother were in the process of writing 'thank-you' cards when the sergeant rang the doorbell. The captain gave them a nice compliment, saying that in the future, when my parents would reminisce upon the week of the wedding, they should remember her and not me.

Having a crystal ball, it might've been the better choice to resign.

But, with my reputation on the line, I noticed a tangled vine within just reach that I was convinced was strong enough to pull me out of the abyss.

That untested third sample.

If my third sample was clean, as it had to be, then it would prove that the two positive results were either tainted, or they came from someone else.

But if I surrendered that night, it would all become moot, as the Medical Division at Lefrak would throw the evidence away, and I would never know the truth.

I refused, and again asked to go home.

"If you do need help," he said to me, with concern in his eyes as we left his private office, "don't hesitate to reach out and contact me."

"I appreciate the offer, but I've got a long fight ahead of me," I responded. "I just wish that there was something that I could say to prove to you that I didn't do it."

"Let's just agree to disagree."

"Fair enough," I said, drained.

No more tonight, I said to myself.

Save your strength for tomorrow.

I was asked to have a seat once again, to wait while the Captain arranged my escort back to the Bronx. Besides courtesy, he also needed to collect my remaining firearms, currently at my private residence.

Waiting patiently, I glanced up at a poster-sized, framed photograph hanging on the wall in front of me. It was an aerial shot of an entire class of Academy graduates, standing at attention on the Garden floor, captured forever in mid-salute.

Again, I saw the proud white doves, this time from a new perspective, and the tears that were absent for most of the night finally arrived in full force.

I've never cried like that before, and I doubt I ever will.

Thus, at 0005 hours - or five minutes after midnight - on March 17, 1999, I was officially suspended without pay for failing an end-of-probation drug examination.

The lieutenant on the desk at the 46th precinct was notified a few minutes later, and word of my betrayal probably spread from the desk to the patrol supervisors to the midnight platoon. Considering how rumors are like wildfire, the midnight platoon might then inform the day tour, and the day tour would inform the four to twelve. By the time IN-TAC called the Four-Six to find out why I was missing the following day, an entire precinct of four hundred cops would be buzzing over the new hot topic, with a wild spectrum of theories and opinions.

However, they would all share one thing in common - an association between my name and illegal drugs.

By the end of the week, the tally would likely be in the thousands, as an official department-wide memo regarding the dole exam would circulate to the desks of every single command, in every borough of the city.

Before the first battle had even begun, my war was already lost.

SIX

Ninety percent boredom, ten percent terror.

One of my Academy instructors said that about police work, and he was right.

Documentary police shows on television would have you believe that the percentage swings heavily in the other direction, but that's just not the case.

To create a typical episode, they take a videographer and throw them in the back of a radio motor patrol — an RMP — while a team of cops drive around for days, sometimes even weeks, before they stumble across something interesting enough to put on TV.

During the time in between, the officers in question simply wait. They get coffee, they talk about sports and the opposite sex, and they respond to emergency calls that are either unfounded or unnecessary or gone on arrival.

However, it's only a matter of time before a situation explodes around them, and the terror begins.

Ninety-ten. Even in the most crime-ridden places, the ratio never swings much more than 85-15.

The 46th precinct in the Bronx, however, was one such place.

Located two blocks off the Grand Concourse, the Four-Six is actually a very small precinct. Responsible for a little over a square mile of territory - only one-fortieth of the total size of the entire borough - it stretches from Fordham Road to 175th Street traveling north-south, and from Webster Avenue to University Avenue east-west, with a few oddly-shaped areas incorporated into its perimeter.

However, pound-for-pound, it remains one of the busiest chunks of real estate in the entire city.

The front of the building was unremarkable, a grid of simple red bricks bordered by light gray mortar and a short platform of stone steps that led to a tall archway, about fifteen feet high. Two thick oak doors on each side of the entrance parted in the middle to allow access to the interior. On my way up those steps and inside, a uniformed cop halted me in my tracks.

"Can I help you?" he asked me, blocking my progress. He was about my age, but the leather goods on his duty belt showed some wear. He recognized my blank stare and continued.

"You must be one of the new guys," he said with a grin, quickly moving aside. "Go ahead. The sergeant at the desk will tell you where to go."

Either unaware of my presence or not interested enough to look up, the desk sergeant presided over several haphazard piles of paper and made entries in an oversized textbook, while a female in glasses seemed to watch his penmanship and read a newspaper simultaneously.

"What do you want?" the female asked, looking me up and down. As ordered, I was dressed in civilian attire, with my uniform and gear in a suit bag slung over my arm.

"Reporting from the Academy for orientation," I responded. She was a Hispanic woman in her thirties, with olive skin and dark hair wrapped in a tight ponytail. She pointed to an adjacent hallway that ended with a door.

"Go in there," she commanded, and resumed her double reading.

It was yet another classroom, complete with plastic chairs and a chalkboard. Twenty-one rookies in total, all with ants in their pants, eager to officially begin their careers. Of course, we were students still, and for another two days PBA reps and supervisors and cops from the previous class would talk to us, about safety and precinct conditions and where to get the best chicken parm sandwiches.

And we would remain students afterwards, as there would always be more to learn.

However, it was finally time to work.

***

The iron fire escape that extended from the building would provide some protection from falling objects, but it was far from perfect. If someone decided to pour liquid from one of the many windows, or maliciously drop a balloon or an egg, I would be defenseless against it. The metal landing would most likely keep me safe from solid items, but the cleanliness of my uniform was an entirely different matter.

This was the least of the long list of concerns darting through my head as I walked with another rookie on Davidson Avenue between 174th and 175th Streets, a drug-infested block located within the confines of the 46th precinct.

There were many foot post assignments in my first six months at the Four-Six. Our entire training group was placed in a separate squad and ordered to report at five-thirty P.M., five days a week. We were the excess manpower, the overflow, used for a variety of functions. The members of Club Twenty-One spent tours guarding corpses in empty apartments until the medical examiner would arrive in his van with his black plastic zipper bags to drag the bodies unceremoniously off to the city morgue. Other times, we sat and watched the minutes crawl along in hospital rooms, baby-sitting injured prisoners until they received a clean bill of health, so that we could usher them back to jail. But when there was nothing specific to do with us, the men above told us to take our equipment and grab a portable radio and stand on a cold, uneventful corner.

Ninety-ten, 85-15.

My very first experience with the fifteen was while driving a sergeant. His responsibilities were to cruise the precinct, monitor the radio, and make routine checks on his people. My task was to drive the car, a glorified chauffeur. However, it was rare for a rookie to get a car tour, so it was a good opportunity to learn the command and its boundaries.

That particular sergeant was a tall, authoritative man with an odd-looking mustache. It was in the shape of an upside-down "U," running over his upper lip and down the sides of his face, along with a shaved chin. It was common knowledge throughout the house that he was a Civil War buff, and it was believed that his facial hair was an extension of that hobby. According to rumors, his weekend getaways consisted of sprinting through the woods in full Union foot soldier regalia, reenacting the famous battles of America's past. He carried himself on patrol with such confidence that such stories only enhanced his reputation, to the point that the station house suffered a mild outbreak of unauthorized 'Fu-Man-Chus.'

It happened at eight o'clock, or 2000 hours, according to a new method that I was required to use to tell time. While randomly cruising in and out of one-way streets that I had never seen before, my radio made a strange sound, a whining that raised the hair on the back of my neck. From my point of view, the female voice that followed the alert was inaudible, but her tone displayed a sense of urgency that I had recognized from my short month at the North.

Fortunately, the sergeant, a twelve-year veteran, would have understood the transmission had his portable been locked in the trunk.

He reached for the terminal between us and began frantically pushing buttons. Suddenly, the red and white turret lights and the horn on the roof flooded the area with color and sound.

"What's going on?" I asked him.

"You didn't hear?" he answered, incredulously. He grabbed the megaphone off the dashboard and began barking orders to vehicles to move out of the way.

"Gun run," he said.

Without conscious thought, my gas pedal foot grew heavier. I didn't hear the address, but the sergeant assumed that I hadn't learned the precinct yet and shouted basic directions. I felt a rush of adrenaline surge through me like the current from a wall socket. The dispatcher chimed in with additional information, and this time, I understood.

"Shots fired, 1900 Grand Concourse, between Echo Place and East Tremont. Anonymous complainant states that there are five to seven males with guns on the roof of that location. No descriptions, no callback. Is Four-Six Charlie on the air?"

"Six Charlie red," the requested sector car confirmed, over the radio. The name "Charlie" stood for the letter "C," which was the title for two cops assigned to a particular car that night. It was common practice to use names instead of the alphabet over the radio, to avoid confusion. "Show us responding."

Other anxious units followed with transmissions of their own.

"Six Henry on the back..."

"Six George is also going over there, Central."

As I drifted through a red light cautiously and slammed on the accelerator, my intense passenger keyed his portable. "Central, Six Sergeant One is also en route."

With left-and-right directions, it took us all of thirty seconds to reach the building. Two other royal blue and white RMPs were already parked on the sidewalk outside, with a third sector tailgating us. As I skidded to a stop and shoved the gearshift into park, the Civil War enthusiast jumped out of the vehicle and bolted for the entrance full-speed. I chased after him, trying to clear my mind and harness the fear that was slowly engulfing me. As the sergeant and I reached the doorway, a lone man was exiting. In his late forties, he was of obvious Latin descent, with a light beard.

To both his and my apparent shock and bewilderment, my boss grabbed him by the front of his shirt and pushed him violently against the metal door, in my general direction.

"Toss him!" he commanded as other cops rushed past us and into the lobby. He had used a slang term, but one that I understood. "Quickly!"

The man thrust his hands to the sky, offering no resistance. As I patted his abdomen and waist for bulky objects, the sergeant squeezed past us, his Glock aimed at the floor and partially concealed behind his thigh as he moved onward. He bounded up one of the three visible staircases, leaving me behind with my terrified host. Anxious to follow and not finding anything threatening, I apologized and told the man to go. The man said something politely in a foreign language, but I didn't have time to translate. I picked a different stairway and began my precarious ascent alone.

There were five floors. With each landing, the available light decreased. By the fourth tier, I had to take out my flashlight to combat the darkness. I took my time with every level knowing that there could be an enemy around each bend, looking to escape and ready to hurt anyone that stood in their path. And if they were armed with a gun - as advertised - they would have a distinct advantage. A criminal, by definition, has no rules binding the use of his firearm. But for me, it was all rules and no guidance. Unlike the practice line at Rodman's Neck, there would be no tower, no one dressed in khaki slacks to tell me exactly when to draw and cover, no buzzing sound to help make that ultimate, split-second decision.

Too soon, you give up your shield, lose your job, maybe go to prison. Too late, and you die.

Suddenly, I heard muffled yelling, coming from directly above me. With an inexplicable disregard for my own safety, I took the last flight of stairs three at a time, driving my shoulder into an unlocked door on the roof. I was surprised to find the situation firmly under control.

Oddly enough, I was disappointed.

Five males dressed in winter bubble jackets were lying prone, face down on the roof, with their hands clasped behind their heads. Several officers stood in a semicircle with guns drawn, as a single cop knelt down and calmly tossed each suspect, patting and probing them, one at a time. Others continued to search the rooftop with lashing beams of white light, scanning for weapons and additional rivals.

In the final analysis, there were never any guns, neither on the males nor hidden on the roof.

However, the sergeant wasn't finished with them yet.

"Who has the pot?" he said, brandishing a hollowed-out cigar wrapper in his hand. Instead of using paper, pot smokers sometimes rolled marijuana cigarettes with the leaf covering of a cigar. In 1998, it was still illegal to smoke marijuana in New York City.

"That's not ours," one of the men responded. He was the biggest of the group, easily two hundred and fifty pounds. But judging by his voice, he was probably just a large kid, no more than eighteen or nineteen. The sergeant walked over to the boy, leaning over him.

"Are you trying to bullshit me?" he said, threateningly. He placed his military-style combat boot on the man-child's hand, applying weight. The youth squealed in pain.

"Don't lie to me!" the sergeant continued, ranting. "You kids were up here smoking, making a shitload of noise, and the tenants in the building called nine-one-one. When you heard the footsteps, one of you motherfuckers threw the pot over the side. Isn't that right?" He added more pressure, and the teen wailed even louder.

"Isn't that right!?!"

"Yes, yes," the kid answered through clenched teeth, almost sobbing. "We didn't wanna cause any trouble, officer. We were just hanging out."

The sergeant crouched down low, so that the boy could see the intimidating look in his eyes, the unusual horseshoe on his face. "Well, the next time I get a call and I have to run up those fucking stairs again, and I find you and your friends up here, hanging out..." He bent lower, pausing for dramatic effect. "... I'm gonna throw *you* over the side."

After his threat, he told them all to go. They wasted no time, almost running for the exit.

Soon, Mr. Mustache sent the sectors back out on patrol, and we calmly took the elevator back down to our vehicle. When we resumed our aimless cruising of the streets, I had some important questions to ask. Unfortunately, I wasn't quite sure how to phrase them, so I started with idle conversation instead.

"That was my first gun run," I said.

"Most of them are like that," he said, watching cars pass us in traffic. As a cop, they tell you to drive below the speed limit, that way you can view your surroundings better. "You get the call and race over, to find out that it's nothing - a false alarm. Maybe some lady doesn't like the loud music playing in the apartment next door, so she calls the cops, tells the dispatcher that she heard gunfire. I've responded to a thousand of them."

"Were they all false alarms?"

"No."

Silence followed. I saw a group of guys standing on a street corner, leaning against a wall. I found myself examining their waistbands. The boss continued.

"Never take a gun run for granted. You never know when it will be for real. Always approach it like the men on the roof want to kill you. That way, you won't get killed."

"Why were you so hard on that kid?"

"Fear."

I'm sure he could see that I was still confused. I kept quiet and let my teacher collect his thoughts.

"I saw a documentary once, about Death Row inmates, guys who murdered police officers," he began, lowering the volume on the radio. "The interviewers would ask the inmates, 'Why? Why did you do it?' Do you know what most of them said?"

I shook my head, side to side.

"They said, 'The cop did not have control of the situation.' Do you know what that means?"

"No."

I had a glimmer, but it seemed like the right answer at the moment.

"It means that the cop *gave them* the opportunity."

A traffic light turned red, and we sat and waited for the green signal. A Buick idled alongside us, its occupants staring straight ahead, acting like we were invisible.

"Fear eliminates the opportunity," he added, waving me on with his hand. I looked both ways and inched the vehicle through the intersection against the rules, leaving the Buick behind.

"It's not nice, but the city doesn't pay you to be nice. They pay you to go on gun runs and get home safe. If you scare the shit out of him, he's too busy being afraid to figure out a way to hurt you. If you stick a gun in his face and tell him not to move or you'll blow his fucking brains out, then if he *does* have a gun, he won't have a chance to use it. And if he doesn't, you can apologize later and send him on his way. Either way, you go home safe. He'll live through the fear. You might not live through the bullet."

As I stood under the fire escape on Davidson Avenue, I often thought about that sergeant, wishing that I was his regular driver. In my mind, there was no safer companion. Of course, there were also selfish reasons: I wanted the warmth and mobility of the car, the occasional lights-and-sirens adrenaline rush.

Plus, there was a much smaller risk of getting egg yolk on my uniform.

Davidson Avenue had its own economy. Three drug suppliers aggressively competed with each other for new and old customers, all in the span of two city blocks. People from far and wide drove their cars through that poorly lit one-way street to find a familiar face and pull over, to make an exchange - money for a glass vial or a plastic bag - and drive off.

We knew exactly who the street pushers were, but that information mattered very little. To make an arrest, a police officer must witness the actual exchange of currency for drugs. Without that visual evidence, there was no probable cause and no collar. It didn't matter if you knew that Mr. Smith had every pocket brimming with dime bags and eight balls. If you went into Smith's pockets, you would be violating his constitutional right of privacy and disobeying departmental guidelines regarding search and seizure.

Thus, our main purpose was simple police presence. If we were standing on the block where Mr. Smith usually offered his wares, he had no choice but to lay back and let customers drive by. He would lose the sale until I turned my back or hid in a random building to escape the bitter cold, or went on my one-hour meal break.

Thus, they hated us with a passion, because we were bad for business.

If a balloon filled with shaving cream happened to fall out of one of a hundred windows above and splattered on the sidewalk beside me, we all knew why, and there wasn't much we could do about it besides stand strategically under a store awning or a tall, dense tree.

And we would be lucky if it was only shaving cream.

Officer Wilson Rodriguez, also a new guy, stood next to me under that fire escape. He was my occasional training partner, his surname alphabetically on the roll call next to mine. He was a quiet man, someone who never spoke simply to fill the air with sound. This sometimes made working a foot post with him difficult. I needed conversation to fill the time. So I probably talked his ear off, but he didn't seem to mind.

"You gonna take the sergeant's exam when the time comes?" I asked him.

"If I'm still here," he said, through the wool turtle-neck dickey that covered his mouth and chin. It was early January, so we both had an excuse to wear all the optional winter gear that the police equipment shops showcased all year around.

"What do you mean?" I asked.

"I may not stay in the NYPD," he answered, eyeing a seller across the street who was sitting on the stoop of a private house, annoyed and also freezing. "I may take the FBI field exam, go federal."

"Ambitious," I said, looking at the windows across the way, some lights on, some off. "Don't you need a law degree or a Master's degree, or something?"

"Not if you have three years of law-enforcement experience. Or I may go somewhere else. Another department, maybe."

"Somewhere warm, I hope."

"Yeah," he said, staring at a car, parked at the curb in front of us. "How many pieces do you have?"

"None today," I replied. Will was referring to tickets. It was our other responsibility: gathering revenue for the city. The powers above wanted two 'books' a month, or forty tickets total. I had no idea what would happen if I didn't bring in the requested amount, but I didn't want to find out.

"Let's go get some parkers," he suggested.

We went for a walk. The easiest piece for a cop to find on foot patrol is a missing or expired registration or inspection certificate, glued to the front windshield of all New York State motor vehicles. With two rows of parked cars, Will took one side of the street and I took the other.

It was when I was reading the reggie on what would have been my second ticket of the tour that my radio made a sound from under my heavy-duty jacket. It was a loud sound, and very brief.

"What was that?" I said to Will, not looking up from the sticker on the windshield yet.

"I'm not sure," he said, unhooking the portable from his belt and holding it against his ear.

"I think I heard someone... yell."

"Is there a unit trying to reach Central?" the dispatcher said over the radio, also wondering about the sound.

"Do a run-down," the Civil War sergeant commanded over the air, cruising around somewhere. A 'run-down' was a method of determining the identity of a unit on patrol. The central dispatcher would hail every sector and foot post on her frequency, one at a time. When they called us, Will keyed his radio and made a quick acknowledgment.

All of the units answered, except for one.

"Six Post Twelve? Six Post Twelve, please respond," the female voice said over the air, waiting for a reply.

Nothing but silence.

"What's the location of that unit?" the sergeant impatiently asked Central.

According to Central, Post Twelve was on a family dispute, and she quickly read the address and apartment number of their location from her computer screen. As I began swiftly walking with my partner, I thought about the names of the two officers assigned to Twelve that night, both rookies and new acquaintances - Kirk Boeing and Robert Ordonez.

Kirk was very thin and tall, at least six-foot-four, and had wheat-like, short blonde hair, earning him the nickname "Big Bird" from his peers. I had met him late in the Academy in the 'Tac House,' a training facility on the outskirts of Rodman's Neck that consisted of cheap plywood and makeshift stage settings. I remember watching in awe from the railing above as Big Bird took a fake gun from the waistband of an angry 'alcoholic.' I had worked with him a few times already, always finding a way to learn something from him.

Ordonez, on the other hand, had no catchy nickname, but he was no less memorable. Bobby's locker was in the same row as mine at the station house, and we had already begun a friendly war over the local baseball teams. I liked the Yankees, and he was a lifelong Met fan. I had worked a foot post with him the previous week and our debate raged throughout the tour, banishing the tedium.

Despite numerous hails, their voices were silent over the radio, unaware or unable to respond.

With radio in one hand, eight-point cap in the other, and twenty-five pounds of gear strapped to our waists, we sprinted up and down concrete hills and valleys like men possessed. After about ten blocks or so, I felt the customary stitch in my side. It was further away than I realized, as the address of the dispute was at the opposite end of University Avenue. But even though the first sector was already pulling up to the apartment, stopping to rest was not an option.

It was unthinkable.

As we reached a main intersection, two RMPs roared past us, lights and sirens. A third vehicle trailed about two or three seconds behind. Suddenly, they screeched to a halt and waited for us to lumber forward. We dove into the back seat and they launched off again like a rocket. My lungs screamed for oxygen, my heart was ready to burst, and that universal fight hormone - adrenaline - pulsed through my body, like never before.

Luckily for everyone, I would be disappointed once again.

As it turned out, Bobby and Big Bird were fine. They had responded to that dispute to find a husband and wife in the midst of a heated argument. Concerned neighbors had heard the ruckus and made the call. To play marriage counselors, they lowered the volume on their portables, not hearing our repeated hails. By the time we were rushing up the front steps, the tense event had already become a laughing matter.

That night, Will and I hitched a ride back to the command, to sign out. The two veteran cops in the sector talked to us at length, treating us like equals. I remember standing on the roll call line with a pen in hand, joking with Kirk about the chaos that he and Bobby had caused. Once upstairs, I went to my locker, spun the combination, and began peeling off the multiple layers in silence. When I was slipping into my civilian clothing, Bobby finally said something to me that I will never forget.

"You're a good guy," he told me.

"We didn't do anything that anyone else wouldn't do," I said.

"No, in general," he added, pulling his turtleneck over his head. "When I first met you, I thought to myself: 'What's this guy's angle? Why is he so... nice? Then I realized you don't have an angle. That's just the way you are."

I smiled, appreciative but uncomfortable with the unexpected praise. Bobby continued.

"I know you and Will were on foot tonight, on Davidson. I know how far away that is... Thanks for coming."

"Anytime," I replied, silently wondering why I was uneasy.

It wasn't until the next day at the station house that I understood my mixed emotions, and also why most cops run to the location when the radio speaks.

That night, I didn't run to save Bobby, or Kirk. I felt guilty because my seemingly altruistic act had very little to do with either of them.

I realized that I had run to save myself.

It could have been me on the opposite end of that transmission, alone against the enemy, desperate for help. If the day came that I truly needed a 'ten-thirteen,' and I was only able to scream out my location before plunging into battle, I wanted to hear the sound of sirens in the distance, growing louder with each passing moment.

I wanted to know that Kirk and Bobby and the rest of the blue warriors would be there, willing to fight alongside me.

So, if I wanted them to run for me, then I would have to run for them.

Eventually, I rose from the comfort of the couch in the precinct lounge, with a sole purpose in mind. Near the stairwell leading to the muster area upstairs was a door, closed but unlocked. I opened it and stood in the doorway, briefly glancing around. The room was empty, except for basic gymnasium equipment - mostly dumbbells and ancient cardio machines.

I looked at the timekeeper on the far wall. Four o'clock.

There was still some time left. I stepped onto a treadmill and pushed a few buttons, and the conveyor belt beneath me began to move.

With only my conscience to keep me company, I ran with a familiar intensity, right up until I had to put on my uniform and go visit Davidson again.

***

Ironically, my most difficult decision on the job did involve illegal drugs.

However, it wasn't in a way that you might think.

But first, a character introduction.

Frank Sumner, a Four-Six veteran, was a very funny guy.

He drove the van that carried all the prisoners to Bronx Central Booking, a non-patrol assignment that was his bone to chew, exclusively. Any night that he worked, it would be his responsibility to transport the perps. But considering the high volume of arrests within the precinct between the hours of five P.M. and two A.M., no one person could be expected to handle this task alone.

Thus, Frank was given an additional job by default, that of kiddie counselor.

The platoon commander would assign two different rookies every tour to join him and his prisoners, as extra sets of eyes and hands. And on those trips, Frank would entertain with outlandish stories from his past, of on-the-job adventures that had made the transition from terrifying to hysterical through that strainer called time.

On days when I was told by a boss that I had "Prisoner Transport," I knew that it was a virtual lock for a pleasant evening.

As usual, I stood with the rest of our training group for roll call at five o'clock, or 1700 hours. My partner for that night was Tommy Pasano, an Irish-looking guy with whom I had shared many a foot post with, again due to the proximity of our names alphabetically on the roll call. We happily reported to Frank upon learning of our assignment, and he promptly told us to go downstairs and play Ping-Pong. It was practical for him to wait until the precinct holding cells were choked with "skells," to deliver them en masse to Central Booking, which was located on 161st Street, a few blocks from Yankee Stadium. That way, Frank and his helpers made the fewest number of trips.

We made three such trips on that infamous night. The first one was at 1800 hours. We made our initial drop off, after which we snuck off to Little Italy in the bordering Four-Eight for an unaccountable pasta dinner, then returning to take full advantage of our on-the-books one-hour "meal" in the basement. Then at about 2100, we made another uneventful trip. We returned home at midnight, or

100

0000 hours, to find the precinct jammed with new criminals. Our tour was officially over at 0205, just enough time for a third and final trip, with perhaps a chance for an hour of overtime for the three of us.

As a prelude to the third run, Tommy and I were required to round up the cattle. Similar to our previous two deliveries, we took each them out of the cell and frisked them again. Our search was just a final brush-over, to make absolutely certain that they were free of weapons or contraband. Then, we handcuffed them to a long chain that held the entire group together, archaic but necessary to keep any single person from developing any notions of escape. There was one female in our group, so we attached her to the last pair of cuffs on the chain, to create some sitting distance from the males while riding in the back of the van.

With the chain shuffling past the main desk, we retrieved our firearms from the safety locker and met Frank outside, who was already behind the steering wheel. As we approached the sliding door of the van, Frank waved me over.

"Check the back," he said to me, referring to the area where the prisoners would sit in transit.

Tommy held the line, and I climbed inside. It was very dark in the rear, so I took out my flashlight. I quickly scanned the floor area with my light, then peered into the crevasse behind the benches that lined the walls.

No weapons, no contraband.

We led them to the back and sat them down, positioning the female away from the rest of the bunch. Content with their safety, I slid an interior door closed, to separate the perps from the three of us. Frank began weaving a tale, something about Irish women and breast size, and nothing about this particular trip seemed remotely out of the ordinary.

That is, until about halfway to 161st Street, when one of the prisoners spoke.

"Officer," he called out, from behind the interior door. "I think you should take a look at this."

I stood up and peered through a gated hole in the partition. "What is it?" I asked, squinting.

From my vantage point, it was too dark to see anything. I had no choice but to get up from my perch.

Armed again with my flashlight, I slid the door aside and stumbled into the rear of the vehicle, trying to keep my balance as the van lurched over bumps and potholes. The vocal perp motioned to a small object resting on the floor. I shined my light.

In the center of what was an empty floor ten minutes earlier was four tiny, plastic tubes, no bigger than three inches long, all held together by a rubber band.

I picked them up, twirling the little containers between my fingers, inspecting the yellowish-white contents within, three or four tiny crystalline pebbles in each. I wasn't a chemist, but it was fairly obvious.

102

Illegal drugs.

I looked around at my seven passengers, all in
handcuffs, hands firmly locked behind their backs. It could
have belonged to any one of them, perhaps wiggled out
from a side pants pocket. I could have inquired, but that
would have been a waste of time. I returned to the front and
approached Frank with the vials inside a closed fist.

"I have something to show you," I said to him,
opening my hand.

He immediately took the tubes and hid them in a
front pocket. He put a single finger to his lips, the universal
sign for silence, mouthing a message loud enough for me
and Tommy to hear, but not our guests: "Not until we drop
them off."

Bronx Central Booking was an inefficient place, and
probably still is. Luckily, Frank had the process down to a
science, and we were back in the van in less than an hour.
He avoided his normal shortcuts, as he would need extra
time to explain our unexpected situation, to lay out all of
our cards on the table.

He took the illegal tubes out of his pocket as a
visual reminder, and held them in his fingertips.

"We have two options, men," he began, all of the
customary humor missing from his voice. "And,
unfortunately, there is no 'right' answer. One, we bring the
vials back to the desk and voucher them."

"And the other option?" Tommy asked, beating me to the punch.

"We throw them down a sewer drain."

The van squealed to a halt at a red light, and the big boat rumbled and spit and coughed while we waited patiently for the light to turn green. I decided to interrupt the uneasy silence.

"What do you want to do?" I asked Frank, naturally looking to him for leadership. After all, he had seniority, and he was the pilot.

"It's not what I want to do," he responded, smirking in an apologetic fashion. "It's what *you* want to do."

"Me?" I said, surprised. "Why me?"

"You found it," he answered, spinning the wheel around an odd-shaped turn. Judging from our surroundings, he was taking the scenic route. "It's your call."

"What *should* I do?" I asked them both, seeking guidance. Honestly, in my head, I had already made a preliminary decision, to throw the vials into a plastic security envelope and type out a property voucher, but it couldn't hurt to ask.

"It's not for me to say," Frank replied, looking at me more than the road. "I'm just a cop, like you. I don't have a chevron on my sleeve."

"Let's voucher it then," I said.

"Not a bad decision," he answered, sounding as if he were about to spin one of his trademark tales. "Obviously, the little critters were hidden in one of the skell's pockets. While we were headed over to Central Booking, he probably reached around, pulled them out with his fingers, and dropped them on the floor. Vouchering the drugs is definitely not the wrong thing to do. But if you do decide to go that way, someone might get hurt."

"How?" Tommy asked.

"Well, if the drugs were on the body of one of the perps, and we found them in the van, then that means that the arresting officer and his partner overlooked them at the scene. Then, those same two cops obviously missed the drugs again when they tossed the perp in front of the desk. If we voucher them... they get in trouble."

A light bulb suddenly appeared above my head. "But waitaminute, Frank — there were *seven* prisoners. There would be no way to assign blame to any one sector or foot post. How would they know who missed the drugs?"

"Very true," he responded, pulling into the parking lot of a Dunkin' Donuts. All stereotypes aside, it was one of the few places that was open twenty-four hours, and they had great coffee. "But let me ask you something: Who had the responsibility of tossing the perps a third and final time, just before they left the precinct?"

"Oh God," Tommy said, with a look of nausea slowly creeping onto his face. I was also beginning to feel it. "Us."

"If one of you had discovered the vials back at the house," Frank continued, speaking slowly, administering advice with a teaspoon, "we could have simply added it onto the guilty skell's OLBS as another charge, and it would have been no big deal." He was referring to the On-Line Booking Sheet, one of the many arrest forms. "But now, it's messy. For the lack of a scapegoat, they might give the three of us CDs. Keep in mind, I've gotten Command Disciplines before. But I'm not on probation. You guys are."

Tommy finally lost it. "I can't believe this," he exclaimed, running his hands vigorously through his hair. "We should've stripped those fucking guys naked before we left the precinct." He rocked back and forth in his seat, visibly shaking.

"Why do I have a feeling that Option Number Two isn't going to be all that pretty?" I said to Frank as the vehicle came to an abrupt stop near the entrance of the coffee shop. Standing up, I nearly lost my balance. I hoped my grasp on the situation was more secure.

"You have good instincts," Frank answered, turning the engine off. "If you choose Number Two, and decide to throw it down a sewer, then the arresting officer and his partner are clear and so are we. No one will ever know, except for the three of us, and God. But there is something else to consider."

"What?" Tommy asked, his voice laced with desperation.

"What if it's a test?"

106

"A test?" I asked, confused.

From whom? For what reason?

Obviously, I wasn't thinking clearly, because there could only be one answer, even back then.

The Internal Affairs Bureau.

"I've seen it happen," Frank continued, doing what he did best, relating yet another story. "An agent for IAB walks up to a cop on patrol, hands him a wallet with a $20 bill inside. Tells him that he found it sitting on a sidewalk somewhere. If the cop neglects to voucher the wallet - or vouchers it twenty bucks lighter - he comes to work the next day to find out that he's out of a job."

"What does that have to do with us?" Tommy asked.

"Who's to say that IAB didn't make a visit to the Four-Six a few hours ago, slide open the door of the van while we were in the house playing Ping-Pong, and drop drugs into the back of the van? *These* drugs." He again showed us the contraband, dwarfed in his monstrous palm. Frank was a giant; at least six-foot-three, weighing three hundred pounds on a generous scale.

Could the drugs have been on the floor, and I missed them? I was reasonably sure that they were not there, but I had never been one to gamble, not when the stakes were so high.

Then, another horrible idea sprang into focus. *What if one of the perps in the van was never arrested in the first place, but was working undercover for IAB?*

Frank concluded his pitch, in a neat and tidy fashion. "If this *is* a test, and you *don't* voucher them... then you *definitely* lose your job."

"Tommy," I said, almost pleading, as we drove around the block of the station house, stalling, acting as if we were searching for a parking spot, "don't you have an opinion?"

"I don't know, Chris," he replied, curled over in his seat. "Seems like we get screwed either way."

Impulsively, I came to a decision.

"Let's throw the damn thing away," I blurted out.

Frank quickly double-parked near a corner, letting the engine run.

He handed me the vials, which I held tightly in my palm.

"Do it fast, so that no one sees you," he said in a hushed tone.

I jumped down from the van and walked over to the sewer.

Then, taking a moment to stare at the hundreds of dark windows surrounding me on all sides, I realized that Frank was wrong.

108

There was, in fact, a right answer.

Taking a deep breath, I returned to the van, having never opened my fist.

Frank drove a few blocks, finally finding a parking spot.

I was exhausted, mentally and physically, but my conscience was finally at ease.

When I opened my hand again, it was to drop the vials onto the sergeant's desk, to voucher the drugs.

Nothing ever came of it, and I have no regrets.

***

I was never a hero.

There was a short period of time, as I was driving around in a sector car on a semi-regular basis, that I wanted nothing more than to 'rip steel from a man's waistband,' as the old police saying goes. But I never made a gun collar.

I didn't have all that many arrests, either. My limited history was a collage of domestic disputes, blade-wielding assaults and Orchard Beach DWIs. Right before IAB contacted me, I was on the verge of receiving a bottom-rung medal — an Excellent Police Duty - for an arrest that was more good fortune than good police work.

Club Twenty-One had been at the command for only three months at the time of that particular arrest. I had been assigned to a foot post, strolling the length of Morris Avenue, around 182nd Street. It was a warm afternoon in January, and the streets were brimming with people. They sat on apartment building steps, listening to rap and reggae on competing car radios, leaning on the metal pull-down gates of storefronts that were either closed or permanently out-of-business. Of course, some of them had an illegitimate purpose for being outdoors, but the nice weather was still the main reason for the heavy turnout.

I remember feeling desperate. It was still early, but I had no summonses for the month yet, and I was afraid of falling behind and incurring the wrath of Mustache Man or other bosses with bigger shields. I told myself that I absolutely had to get at least one ticket, even if we had to hike cross-precinct to find it.

As it turned out, I would not have to walk very far at all.

There was a group of young males, hanging out in front of a graffiti-blanketed building. One of them held an open glass container, wrapped in a brown paper bag. I took the initiative and approached them.

"What are you drinking, sir?" I asked him, reaching for the bag and gently taking it out of his hand. I had posed the question only to be polite. Through trial and error, I had

110

learned that sometimes the best course of action was to just take action. Besides, it was also a safety issue. He could have decided to break said bottle over my head, if things went sideways.

I had no idea how realistic a possibility that actually was, considering that I had just stumbled across an outstanding warrant on the run.

"It's not soda, officer," he replied, smiling. From his tone of voice, I could tell that he was only trying to be funny, not disrespectful. It was a half-finished bottle of Colt .45 Malt Liquor.

He probably had no clue that he was about to go back to jail. Then again, neither did I.

"Do you have any ID on you?" I asked, secretly ecstatic. I had my elusive piece for the day. I was getting greedy, already thinking about number two.

"No, I'm sorry, officer - I don't," he replied.

At that point, I was already taking out my cuffs. "Well, I do have to write you a summons, for the beer. Since you don't have identification, I have no choice but to take you back to the station house." Without hesitation, I gently grabbed his shoulder and faced him toward the brick wall, beginning a pat down.

He offered no resistance, but did voice a confused protest.

"Is this really necessary?" he asked as his friends watched in shocked silence.

"I'm sorry, but it's procedure," I told him, turning him around to face me. "Everyone who rides in a police car must wear cuffs. Do you have someone that can bring your ID to the precinct? Family, maybe?"

"I think so," he answered, his expression growing uneasy.

"Then don't worry about it," I said to him. Honestly, I felt bad for him. "I need to prove who you are. Once I do, I'll write the ticket, and in an hour, you'll be hanging out with your friends again."

Thus, with an official arrest time of 1621 hours from Central, I called for transport and the two of us went for a short ride, back to home base. The patrol supervisor, a heavy Latin guy, reassigned my partner to another foot post. When I arrived at the precinct, I brought my new friend to the desk and emptied his pockets in front of the boss. He threw a pedigree sheet at me wordlessly, then returned to his endless scribbling.

"What's your name?" I asked him.

"Kelvin," he responded.

"Is that your last name?"

"No. My last name is... Monroe."

112

I continued to ask him questions, completing the rest of the sheet. He gave me his social security number, fumbling with the last few numbers, but that was common. I didn't think too much about it at the time.

"Give me a telephone number of someone who can bring in ID for you," I told him, putting his personal stuff back in his pockets.

"I don't know anybody who can do that," he answered.

"Ouch, that's no good," I said, playing a mind game. "You're gonna sit in the cell until someone comes in with proof of your identity. How long do you want to stay here?"

It was just a bluff. At some point, the desk officer would have ordered me to just write the damn ticket and get Kelvin the hell out of his station house. But the extra pressure worked perfectly.

"Um... my aunt can, but I think she's at work." He recited a telephone number, which I wrote on a piece of scratch paper and gave to the T/S, who happened to be Bobby Ordonez.

"Officer, do me a favor," I said to Bobby, handing the completed pedigree to the DO. "Call this number and ask someone to come down to the station house with proper ID for Mr. Monroe, please." My friend nodded affirmatively as I led Beer Man to the holding area, to remove the handcuffs and put him in the cell.

113

When I returned to the main desk, Bobby informed me that he had successfully contacted the aunt, and that she was on her way. I thanked him and went behind the desk to find a lonely computer terminal, to do the warrant check. The grouchy female assistant desk officer granted her assistance reluctantly.

"Nothing," she said after typing in his name and social into the criminal database.

"You mean he's clean?" I asked, eager to get my memo book and write the ticket.

"I didn't say that," she snapped, looking at me with genuine displeasure. "When I type in *this* name and *this* social, I get no criminal record... How old is he?"

"Twenty-nine," I replied.

"You brought him in here," she said, squinting through wire-rimmed glasses. "You found him breaking the law on One-Eight-Two and Morris, he's almost thirty years old, and he has no criminal record. Doesn't that sound a little odd to you?"

It was a rhetorical question, but I understood her point. My best choice was to hold him and wait.

A half-hour later, Bobby sent a message via the precinct intercom that I had visitors. I returned to the main level to find a middle-aged black couple waiting in the complaint room. They introduced themselves as Kelvin's aunt and uncle. I explained the situation, and they provided

114

a photo identification card, belonging to their nephew. They mentioned that Kelvin had lived in Boston until six months ago, temporarily visiting family in the Bronx. This was all news to me, as well as some of the details on the ID card.

For instance, it listed his name as:

"KELVIN PARKER."

"Kelvin told me that his last name was 'Monroe,'" I said, wondering if they might have an explanation. They had none.

Auntie cracked a smile, so I asked her if anything was funny.

"'Monroe' happens to be my maiden name," she said, shrugging her shoulders.

I thanked the couple, telling them that it was not necessary for them to stay, that I had their telephone number and would give them a call when the investigation was complete.

Immediately, I attacked the computer again, typing in the new name.

The machine churned out a long list of 'Parkers,' one of which had a social security number almost identical to the one that he gave me, except for the ninth and final digit, which was one number off. I selected that particular entry. Three pages of green-colored codes and abbreviations scattered themselves over a jet-black background.

I dreaded the ensuing conversation, but I was in over my head. I asked the ADO to translate.

"You might something good here," she said to me, the first words that I had ever heard from her that didn't sound condescending. She called a sergeant over, the same heavy Spanish guy now in the house on a personal break, to look at the monitor.

"How'd you get this guy again?" the supervisor asked me, his eyes still fixed on the screen.

"Open container in public," I said.

"Write this phone number down," he ordered me, pointing to a number on the screen with a long distance area code. "Ask them to put you through to the detectives. Get someone over there to verify this information."

I was still in the dark and embarrassed about it, but I had no choice.

"Sir," I began, cringing. "What do I have?"

He smiled. "You caught a rapist, kid. He's wanted for not appearing in court, on a rape charge."

According to the sergeant, Kelvin was now property of the Massachusetts State Police, and it was our job to notify them to pick up their human cargo at Central

Booking. I made the call, arranging it for the following day. As I sprinted around the station house like a kid on sugar cereal, I realized that there was still one important item left on the agenda.

It was time to break the bad news to the guest of honor.

I returned to the holding area, now with a stack of arrest paperwork.

"You got me, don't you?" he said, grinning.

"What are you talking about?" I asked him, playing a different game this time. No reason to show him my cards yet. For all I knew, Mr. Parker was about to confess to something bigger.

"You *know*..." he replied, dropping his head into his hands.

"Is there something you wanna tell me?"

"Nah," he answered, seemingly resigned to his fate. "How'd you find out?"

"Computers," I answered. "You can't get away from them."

"I guess so," he said, slowly standing up and walking over to the bars, to lean and grab. "I was hoping you'd just write the ticket... Guess not, huh?"

"Nope... sorry," I said, scribbling information onto several carbon sheets, from his pedigree. A question appeared in my mind, so I asked. "Just curious... If you knew, why didn't you run?"

"I thought about it," he said, rubbing his chin. "But you were so quick... Very smooth."

"Smooth?" I asked, smiling.

"Yeah, man," he answered, talking like we were best friends. "You had the cuffs on before I even knew what was goin' on. I thought of running, but you talked me out of it. I actually believed that I'd be back with my boys in an hour. Oh well..."

That night, I spent some time getting to know Kelvin. His version of the story was simple: She was a girlfriend, they broke up, they got back together, and then she made a rape accusation. He insisted that it was consensual. When he didn't show up to court, they issued a warrant for his arrest.

When I handed off my last piece of paperwork, the Latin sergeant, again in the house and talking on a nearby telephone, waved me over.

"I have the AP on the phone. Your collar might be in the newspaper tomorrow," he told me.

Essentially, I knew I was the kid at the birthday party that broke the piñata on his first blind swing. Still, I was pumped when my alarm clock went off the next

118

morning, as I dragged myself out of bed and crawled to the corner store for a cup of coffee and the Daily News.

And there it was, halfway down on the tenth page. The bold headline read:

"BEER RAP ENDS IN RAPE ARREST." **

I went to work that day, slightly uneasy. Every tour, veterans manhandled dangerous people on Morris Avenue and received no recognition for their efforts. As fate would have it, my assignment that day was 'Post Eleven,' or station house security. My job was to stand on the front steps and monitor traffic in and out of the heavy wooden doors. Throughout the tour, cops came and went, voicing their opinions.

All in all, at the Four-Six, it was just another collar. Undoubtedly, my little moment of fame was a decent start, but it wasn't much more than that.

However, in the eyes of my civilian friends, the article was a big deal.

On my next night off, they insisted that we all go out to the local bar. They bought me drinks throughout the evening, asking questions about life on the streets, like I was an actor in an action movie.

Looking back, I still remember the comments of one particular friend in the bar that night. His name was Lawrence. He lived in Florida on and off, and was visiting New York at just the right time. Actually, he was instrumental in arranging the get-together, purchasing the first round of beers.

"Y'know," he began, heading in an unexpected direction. "I don't see you as a cop."

"Really?" I answered, but in my head, I thought: *Excuse me?*

"Yeah," he said, slurring his words a bit. "You're a writer. I think that - deep down - you signed up to find stories, to enhance your writing."

I shrugged, smiling weakly. I tried to leave it alone, but a defensive comment slipped out.

"Y'know... I worked really hard to be where I am."

"Oh... No doubt," he added, waving a hand in defense. "You became a cop, and a good one, obviously. But you were born to be a writer."

He downed the remainder of his beer, suggesting that we get another round. We rejoined the group and changed the subject, which made me happy.

I appreciated his honesty, but I was convinced he was wrong.

I could always write my little stories, on the side. But now I was a cop, and I was finding it hard to imagine my world without it.

Well, I guess he was right.

** *New York Daily News, January 5, 1998, pg. 10.*

SEVEN

March 17, 1999.

The Next Day.

Imagine, for a moment, that you are in love.

When you first met that special someone, you knew that it was going to be more than just a fling.

A strong relationship develops, one that you believe will stand the test of time.

As the months and years pass, you arrive at the conclusion that, while you may have been touched by love before, this new person has become almost an extension of you, like an appendage or an essential organ, linked to everything that you are and will be.

Now, imagine that that person believed that you were guilty of infidelity, or some other form of betrayal.

Also imagine that that individual had proof of your wrongdoing, clear and convincing evidence that you can't understand yourself, much less explain away.

This is how I felt the next morning, after getting only two hours of sleep.

In the frenzy that was my mind that first day, my road to reinstatement was littered with obstacles, but the edges of the path seemed to be clearly defined.

There were only two possibilities, in a fair and decent world.

Either the hair was tested in error, or it wasn't mine.

It was still early, but I knew that I would have to make dozens of telephone calls, so I left my small bedroom for the kitchen, for a larger work area. I needed a big table, to organize my thoughts and plan a strategy. Even though I had wanted nothing more than to crawl under a rock and die, I had never been more focused in my life.

Again: Either the test was in error, or the hair was not mine.

If it was the test that was at fault, there was only two ways to prove it.

One, I needed to have that optional third sample, presumably locked away with the Medical Division of the NYPD, tested at an independent laboratory.

I couldn't send the third sample to the original lab that tested the first two, because if they had screwed up in the first place, then it was not beyond the spectrum of possibility that they might trash or spike the third batch in order to cover themselves.

Two, I had to arrange to take a new hair test as soon as possible, just in case the third sample somehow turned up positive. In order to accomplish this, I had to locate a hair drug-testing laboratory willing to accept a new sample.

Also, I had to figure out how to establish a proper 'chain of custody' for this additional batch - a way to get the hair from my chest to the door of the testing facility while eliminating suspicion. For instance, if my own new sample tested negative, it would be easy for the Department to say that I had simply mailed in my Dad's hair, or that perhaps I had shaved one of my drug-free dogs.

The untested optional third sample, taken along with the other two on February 26, 1999, was probably filed away in a cabinet somewhere on the sixteenth floor of the Lefrak building, hopefully under lock and key. For the strongest possible case against the city, I needed that third batch to get a negative result. In that instance, it would point to the possibility of an error on the part of the lab technicians that had handled my other two samples.

But even in that scenario, my case was still quite gloomy. It would have been easy for the NYPD to say that the company that they used for testing was more reputable than some random facility that I had found on the Internet.

Without much choice, I switched off that area of my mind, content for the time being just to focus on the plan as hard as I could.

From my perspective, two factors were of the utmost importance: The new test, and time.

If that third sample was somehow positive, then I still would need a clean result. But even in that circumstance, my case would be significantly weaker. My opponents would simply argue that my new sample was only negative because of the time passed. Therefore, the longer that it took for me to arrange a new test, the stronger their argument would be against it.

It was a rickety leg to stand on, and I knew it.

Plus, I had not yet considered the second fork in the road.

Logically, if all three NYPD samples came back positive, then the hair couldn't be mine.

In my mind, such a result could only point to foul play.

For instance, if only two of the original samples were positive, but number three turned up clean, then the blame probably would fall on the shoulders of the testing lab, maybe a crooked technician.

However, if all three batches came back positive, then the finger would point directly back at the NYPD, for reasons unknown.

To prove foul play by the Department, I would need to find a different kind of lab, a facility that could perform a DNA test.

Somehow, I would have to obtain one of the three positive samples and have it sent to the DNA lab, along with another hair sample from my chest under a tight chain of custody.

If the two batches of hair did not match genetically, it could prove that the guilty hair was never from my body in the first place.

And that was my plan.

I made nearly a hundred telephone calls, visited numerous doctors and lab technicians, spent money I didn't have, hacking a path in the direction of the truth, for twenty straight days.

Until I was forced to throw the knife away.

EIGHT

Orchard Beach.

I spent most of my summer there, in 1998.

Strangely enough, I had only visited the Beach two or three times before I became a cop, even though it was a grand total of five minutes away from my house, by car. Actually, that was one of my reasons for putting through the paperwork in the first place.

The Beach, which is located within the confines of the 45th precinct, is also a section of Pelham Bay Park, the largest village green in all of New York City, even bigger than Manhattan's famous Central Park. During the winter, the majority of the Park is quiet and sparsely populated, handled exclusively by the roaming Four-Five sectors. But during the hot summer months, the NYPD would siphon off excess units from Bronx precincts, sending the surplus to the small sub-station hidden behind the cobblestone boardwalk off Section Eight, to report on a daily basis from April until September. Most cops are drafted to the beach, two or three low-seniority rookies from each command, annoyed that they must familiarize themselves with yet another work environment and a new cast of characters.

That is, unless you volunteer for the job.

I noticed the flyer at the Four-Six in early March, stapled to the bulletin board in the muster room on a random day after roll call. From the description on the piece of paper, it seemed like a good deal. Technically, the detail was located within the boundaries of my home precinct, which would normally be a no-no. However, due to a loophole in the residency rule, I was allowed to work there because it was a temporary assignment. I imagined myself rolling out of bed five minutes before roll call, only to enjoy the sun and the surf, and then home by sundown to join Maria for supper like a normal couple.

Before the week was out, I faxed over the application, and my request was quickly approved.

And for one of the few times in my life, the truth was even better than my imagination.

I was a member of the first of two roll calls. My group would stand under the shade of a large tree at 1000 hours to hear our names and assignments leisurely called out, with a second cluster of officers beginning at noon. Then, most of us were given a section of the boardwalk to patrol on foot, but we were free to roam as long as we listened for hails on our radios on an empty point-to-point frequency, without a Central dispatcher. And we had no Central at the Beach because there was virtually no crime.

And there were other great assignments. Two beaten-up RMPs, on loan for the summer from the Four-Five, would cruise around the inner and outer roads of the Park, but they were actually glorified gophers for guys on the boardwalk that wanted food or coffee. There was also another car assignment every weekend, stationed alongside the softball field that marked the entrance to the Beach's next door neighbor, Rodman's Neck, essentially a foot post on wheels. Also, in the area behind Rodman's Neck was the testing site for the NYPD's Bomb Squad. Thus, the Beach would assign two cops to babysit and keep the road clear, giving them an RMP for convenience. With ample snacks and good reading material, it was a decent way to kill a day.

But the absolute best task — by far — had to be the rare boat tour. Every day, the same two veterans would travel to a private marina on nearby City Island to jettison a small motorboat to patrol the water around the Beach, primarily to keep jet skiers under control. During one of my first days at the Beach, they needed a third pair of hands to help drop flotation devices in the water, to mark off a safe swimming area. I was chosen at random, and I had a ball. Luckily for me, I made a good impression. Whenever one was off, I would spend the tour partnered with the other half, floating over the waves and working on my tan.

Regardless of post, we were all given two forty-five minute meal periods, with the option of combining them into one long break. Often, I would remove my gun belt and vest, put a radio in my pocket and throw on a civilian t-shirt. My car waited in the parking lot, for me to climb in and ride home to eat my mother's leftovers and nap in my own bed, all while still on the clock.

On occasion, I would also meet with Maria for lunch, and sometimes more.

I remember driving home one night after work, on one such day.

Unexpectedly, my pager vibrated. I quickly looked at the readout, and it was Maria's home number. I had no cell phone yet, so I was forced to wait until I got home to return the call.

"Chris?" she answered the telephone, her voice soaked with desperation.

"It's me," I said, expecting to hear the sounds of kids playing in the background, but hearing only silence. "Is everything okay?"

"Yes... My mother is babysitting the kids. I have to see you."

"Come over."

When she rang the bell, I led her by the hand into my boyhood room, locking the door behind us. I recognized a familiar longing in her eyes and wasted no time, undressing her in eager silence. We made love, and she cried, and I assumed that they were happy tears.

Afterwards, she told me that she had to return home, that her mother was waiting.

At that moment, I was about as happy as I could be. I had a beautiful girlfriend, a new car, and a great job. Going to the gym, I ran with extra vigor on the treadmill, thankful for my good fortune.

When I returned home, my phone was ringing.

"Hello, sweetie," I said, still unaware that the hammer was about to fall. "Today was phenomenal."

There was a delay, an awkward lack of sound, and then she spoke.

"You didn't read the letter, did you?"

"What letter?" I asked, and then it hit me.

"It's over... isn't it?"

"I am so sorry."

"Where's the letter?" I asked, unsure of how to react.

"It's on your car."

When I went back outside, I noticed a small, folded piece of loose-leaf paper, held against the windshield. I grabbed it and opened the door, to sit and read in privacy.

Dear Chris,

I love you more than words can say, and I always will. In the time that I've known you, you have made me so happy. The thought of telling you this kills me, but I have no choice. I'm going back to my husband. I don't love him, but I'm doing it for the sake of my children. I'm sorry, and I hope that you can forgive me someday.

Yours Truly With Love,

Maria

After a sleepless night, I stood at roll call in a daze the next day, feeling like I had been knocked out in a boxing match.

They gave me "Outer Roads" that morning, one of the car assignments. I had thought about calling in sick, but I figured that I would be better off walking the Beach than wallowing at home in misery.

On any other day, I would have been happy for the RMP, but considering the circumstances, I honestly wanted to be stuck on the boardwalk. I asked my quasi-partner for the summer, a 50th precinct cop named Rick to drive so that I wouldn't be tempted to do anything stupid.

Maria's house was only a few minutes outside Orchard Beach, and I didn't trust myself yet.

However, as fate would have it, we did make a quick trip to buy breakfast and coffee at a train station mini-mart, at the request of other cops on the boardwalk. I sat in the passenger seat and watched people in skimpy outfits walk past as my partner took my money and did the

132

legwork. When Rick returned to the car, I asked him to take a scenic route.

Unbeknownst to Rick, it was also in the direction of Maria's house.

As we slowly drove down her block, a familiar female exited a three-family private house at that exact moment, walking down the front steps of the building, as if on cue.

"Stop for a minute," I told Rick, barely in control of my actions.

"Is that her?" He asked me, as stunned by the coincidence as I was. "Are you sure? You okay?"

"Don't worry," I said, but I knew I was treading on thin ice.

I got out of the RMP and approached her. She seemed clouded, dressed in an ill-fitting sweat suit and her hair a loose mess. To me, she was still perfect.

"What are you doing?" I asked her, looking through dark sunglasses that hid swollen eyes.

Her response was confusing and understandable, both at once.

"I don't know."

We stared at each other in silence.

"He's inside."

Coming to my senses, I returned to the RMP, and Rick drove off.

But my resistance to the enchantment was only temporary.

When we returned to the substation, a seed had already been planted. I went to the Captain's office and knocked on the door.

"Sir, I need the rest of the day off," I told him.

At the Beach, the Captain cared very little if you took the day off from the start, but it was common knowledge that giving out 'lost time' was one of his pet peeves.

"What's the matter?" he asked me, waiting for a poor excuse.

"I'm not feeling well, sir," I said to him, telling the truth. I felt a void in my chest, a hole where the wind sucked through.

"Go ahead," he said begrudgingly, waving his wand at me. *I must look terrible,* I thought to myself as I left, surprised at how easily my wish had been granted. I passed Rick on the way to the locker room.

"You're leaving?" he asked, a look of concern on his face.

134

"Yeah... Come with me for a second."

I headed for my locker, with Rick following close behind. I spun my combination, tearing off my blue shirt and vest, leaving my shield and identification card in the cabinet.

Since I was about to dive headfirst into a career-threatening confrontation, I needed a witness.

"According to department records, I own three guns," I told him, pointing inside my locker. In clear view were my two backups, and my service pistol was on my hip, resting in my duty holster. I unfastened my belt and threw the entire leather apparatus into the metal closet, the nine millimeter included. "I need you to vouch for me - that if anything crazy happens - that all my guns are here, at the substation."

"Then let's do one better," he answered just as I was about to snap the padlock shut. He spun the combination on his own locker and opened the door. "Throw them in here until tomorrow."

I liked his idea better. Even in my irrational state, I knew that if a false allegation was made against me, my weapons would need an alibi. Once he secured his locker, I left the Beach dressed only in my navy blue work shorts and a plain white t-shirt. I jumped into my vehicle, and the trip to Maria's house was quick. Fueled only by my passion, I double-parked the car and walked up the alleyway toward her basement entrance, located on the side of the house.

I rang the bell, and a man I never met answered the door.

"Can I help you?" he asked. He looked to be in his mid-thirties with pale skin and dark hair, and slightly on the portly side. It was the man that I had seen in an old wedding tape that I scanned through one afternoon while Maria was at the store. His name was Nicolas, and we had never met or spoken to each other.

"Is Maria here?" I asked her husband.

At that moment, she appeared from the inner darkness and stood beside him, an exasperated look on her face. Two of their four boys followed, and she immediately told them to go back inside. Once the children obliged, I knelt down before them, as if to propose marriage to both.

"Maria," I said, pleading. "I love you. You're making a mistake. Tell this man how you feel about me."

"How could you do this?" Nicolas asked me, well-composed considering the circumstances. "You come here, in front of my children..."

"You're absolutely right, and I apologize," I told him, quickly standing up. "But until yesterday, I was with this woman almost every day for six months, and I will not just disappear as if I never existed. At least not until she tells me - in person - to go away. I deserve that much."

"Chris, you shouldn't have done this," she said, wearing a strained mask. From the look in her eyes, I could tell that she still needed me. Now, it would be up to her to follow my lead.

She led the both of us up the alley to the rear of the building, away from young eyes and ears. "I'm sorry about the letter," she offered, unable to commit any further. I could see the tears forming. "I should have told you in person. I just couldn't bear it."

After some back and forth, she made her decision more than clear.

"I have to stay with my husband," she said.

And with that, I felt my strength returning. I had made my stand, but the war was over.

"I want to say something," Nicolas said, staring me down. Maria stood alongside us, but at that point, she may as well have been invisible. "My wife made her decision, to stay. Now, I'm going to ask you to never come here again - to leave our family alone — so that we can fix things."

"I will not interfere," I responded.

He held out his hand for a handshake, and I accepted it.

"You will never see me again," I said, and I meant it.

After that, my view of Orchard Beach changed.

Suddenly, I began to notice the negatives, like enduring ninety-five degree weather in Kevlar while trapped inside a cruiser with a broken antenna and no Freon. Or sitting alone on a boardwalk on a random Wednesday fighting the urge to make a useless phone call. Or that unavoidable extra hour of the tour, when the masses conveniently extended the park closing time to their own liking, as we lied over a megaphone about tow trucks being on the way to confiscate vehicles.

The list was longer, but not worth discussing.

Then, three weeks later, out of the blue, my telephone rang.

It was Maria.

"Hello, Chris."

"Hi," I answered, my heart suddenly pounding in my chest. It was the first time I had heard her voice since the confrontation in the alley.

"How have you been?"

"Fine, good," I lied, acting glib. "You?"

"Not so good. I threw Nick out."

Rendered speechless, my gut reaction was anger. *What was all of the heartache for?* I wanted to throw the phone across the room.

Maria quickly continued.

"You were right. Nick and I fought like cats and dogs, from the minute that you walked off... I made a terrible decision."

"Why are you telling me this?" I asked her, furious.

"I just wanted to say that I'm sorry. I know that you may never forgive me. I probably wouldn't. I just hope that someday we can at least be friends."

"Maybe someday we can," I said, biting my tongue. As much as I loved her, the damage had already been done.

"I'm sorry, but I have to go."

And my sour perception of the beach - and of Maria, for that matter - continued for another week, until I found myself on Range Road with a vet that I hardly knew.

Fate again, I suppose.

His name was Gonzalez. Instead of a crappy RMP with no air, he had used some of his Beach clout to get a new Jeep, a loaner from the Four-Five. We sat at the mouth of the Road, listening to FM radio and watching cars navigate the circle.

A popular love song graced the airwaves, which sparked the following conversation.

"You married?" I asked him.

"Yeah," he told me, sipping a bottled water. Gonzalez had a bald head, olive skin, and two hash marks. "And a kid, five years old. What about you?"

"No, no kids. And no woman until I get over the last one."

"Broken heart?"

"Yeah," I sighed, scratching my head. "I was really happy, too. And then she went back to her husband."

"Ouch," he said, grimacing.

We had hours to kill, sitting alone. I went into detail, about how Maria and I met, about her complicated life. I fast forwarded to that afternoon visit, the note on the windshield, and my risky trip to her house.

As it turned out, he had a unique perspective that changed the course of my life for the year that would follow, and perhaps longer.

"When she called to tell you that her husband was gone," Gonzalez asked me, probing. "What did you say?"

"I hung up."

"Why?" he asked, not giving away his position yet.

"Because she had already made her decision, in the alley. She picked him."

"But she was trying to get you back."

"I know."

"Let me ask you a question: Do you still love her?"

"Yes," I said, without hesitation. "With all my heart."

"Do you think she still loves you?"

"Yes. She told me that she does... in front of him."

"Excuse me?" he said, squinting.

"When I showed up at her apartment, I asked her to tell him how she feels about me."

"And what did she say?"

"She said that she still loves me."

"Then you won," he told me, triumphantly.

"I don't understand."

"There's nothing that a woman will not do for her children," he said to me, obviously on Maria's side. "In her mind, it was you against the kids. You'll never win that one. It took her a couple of weeks to wake up and realize her mistake."

141

"You think that I should take her back?" I asked, still afraid to open the door.

"I won't go that far," he said, not wanting to take full responsibility for what he had already made inevitable. "But I will say this: She was yours. Even now, as we sit in this Jeep, she belongs to you."

"How do I know that she won't go back to her husband again?"

"You don't," Gonzalez responded, and then drove home a final point. "But if you let fear stop you from following your heart, you'll live with regret for the rest of your life. You'll be sixty years old, wondering what might have been."

After a few minutes of quiet introspection, I keyed my radio and called the Inner Roads RMP for a bathroom break. After a short delay, I hitched a ride back to Section Eight.

I found a pay phone near a crowded hot dog stand, and rifled through my pocket for a quarter. I followed my heart, and in a few days, life - and the Beach - seemed perfect once again.

But, of course, perfection never lasts.

NINE

Late March, 1999.

The waiting room was empty, except for me and the priest.

Actually, the priest was my guest that morning.

I had gone to Father Kenneth Grade of Saint Benedict's Parish in Throggs Neck, to tell him my story. He wasn't a friend of the family, as I was raised in a non-practicing Christian household. Nevertheless, Father Ken put aside time to listen to my story with an open heart. He said that he believed me, and that he would help my cause in any way necessary.

It was a little after nine A.M. when I picked him up at the rectory. A jovial man, Father Ken was in his late forties, heavy and Irish, with a reddish face and piercing blue eyes. I had two appointments that day, and he had agreed to accompany me on both.

It was my makeshift attempt at a proper chain of custody: A physician would cut hair from my chest in front of the clergyman, seal it inside a pre-addressed envelope destined for a drug-testing laboratory, and Father Ken would personally mail away the sample. Then, when the results came back negative, the priest would testify under oath that the clean specimens had never left his sight, in the trial that I would probably be forced to sue the NYPD to obtain.

According to the PBA lawyer that I had been pestering over the telephone with bizarre questions multiple times a day, it was my only legal option - an 'Article 78,' he called it - since I was not entitled by the normal rules to a department hearing. In addition, I was also faxing letters to countless legal firms that had been offering free consultations in newspaper ads. I assumed that once I was no longer on the job, the police lawyer might be less willing to help me.

The date was March 29th, thirteen days after my surprise visit from the Internal Affairs Bureau. If I had any choice in the matter, I would have had my body tested immediately. But I quickly discovered that the process was not going to be quick, or simple.

On the day that the NYPD originally sampled my chest hair at the Medical Division, they gave out that optional piece of paper that allowed any cop to set aside an extra batch, just in case that they wanted to contest the Department's findings. That document clearly stated that it would be the responsibility of the officer in question to find a laboratory to test that optional sample.

What that paper neglected to mention was how difficult it would be for the average person to accomplish this task.

First of all, in 1999, while there were hundreds of labs that test urine, I was only able to find a grand total of six labs in the entire country that analyzed hair.

Only one of those facilities was located in New York State. Two of the six dealt with corporations only, to open large accounts for groups of employees. The third, conveniently located in Manhattan, was unwilling to test my sample because their own specialists had not extracted the hair. However, they were more than happy to make new arrangements - until they discovered that the sample could not be derived from my bald head, a stumbling block that they flatly refused to overcome. The fourth was the actual facility in California that the NYPD had used, which - for obvious reasons - was out of the question.

Four down, only two left.

Number Five was located in Chicago. Posing as an investigator working on behalf of a troubled cop, I convinced them to accept the NYPD sample through the mail. Seven days earlier - on March 22 — I returned to the Medical Division at Lefrak on the sixteenth floor, to sit in that same auditorium and painfully watch applicants in business attire wait and fill out paperwork, all wide-eyed and hopeful.

Eventually, the Med cop that had originally shaved my chest led me into an adjacent office to stand before a locked file cabinet. Under the close scrutiny of a sergeant, he unlocked the cabinet and withdrew a plain white envelope. I asked to inspect it, and they cautiously handed

145

it over. A familiar serial number was handwritten on the front surface, with clear tape covering the reverse side.

It appeared legit.

If the Department had tampered with my third batch, they had done an expert job of it.

Located in the basement of the Lefrak City Building was a post office. The Med cop and I took the elevator downstairs, with the sealed envelope in hand. In general, they were very pleasant and accommodating. When we reached the service window, I purchased an overnight priority mail envelope, addressing it to the Chicago facility. The Med cop placed the sample inside the blue mailer, along with my instructions and a money order that I was asked to provide. Sealing it in my presence, he handed it off and wished me luck.

According to the lab director over the phone, I would be informed of the results in one week, first by fax, then by traditional first-class mail.

Chop, chop, chop, down went the first cluster of vines on that path toward the truth.

I had not yet received that fax as Father Ken and I sat alone in the doctor's office, to have a new sample sent to Laboratory Number Six, just outside Pittsburgh.

I had made arrangements with a lab technician to ship two hair collection kits to two separate doctors in the Bronx, in the event that the credibility of either doctor was

146

vulnerable in any way. Besides, two clean results certainly had to be more convincing than just one.

Unfortunately, it took all of seven days to coordinate - making the phone calls, setting up two appointments for the same day, one closely following the other on the clock, both on a morning that Father Ken was available to walk and watch in my footsteps.

The first office was on Williamsbridge Road, a local practice that I chose randomly from a list of doctors under my expiring insurance plan.

At a quarter after nine, the receptionist called my name. The doctor, a middle-aged Jewish man, asked me to remove my shirt and lean over a padded chair. Using a dry Bic and no shaving cream, he scraped my torso in front of Father Ken, letting the curly hair fall onto a wide sheet of tissue paper. Dressed in latex gloves, he scooped my remains into the designated plastic bag, sealing it inside a white cardboard box. The doctor handed the container to the priest, and we immediately left for a Fed Ex store, to ship the sample to Lab Six.

Our second appointment was with my family physician, in Parkchester.

We repeated the earlier sterile process, like performing a stage play with a new cast. My family doctor, a thin West Indian gentleman, had an identical white box already in his possession, the other hair collection kit. With my chest running out of lengthy specimens, the nurse plundered my armpit, accidentally biting deep into tender skin with the dry razor. Again, the white box found its way into Father Ken's hands, and we returned to the FedEx office, to mail the hair sample away.

In my mind, I would soon have at least two negative results, long before my thirty-day appeal period was finished. As I drove my new friend back to the rectory, I imagined a bright future where all three tests came back sparkling, and the Department issuing an apology and arranging for my immediate reinstatement.

After dropping him off, there wasn't much left to do except wait. The result of the third sample at Laboratory Five in Chicago was due any day, as the case that I planned to build would begin on that foundation.

Fate, however, would not prolong my suspense.

I had barely left sight of the church before my pager rattled furiously inside my pocket. It was my mother's work number. Immediately, I raced to a nearby payphone with my heart stuck in my throat. The Chicago laboratory had probably sent the results to her fax machine, as the required seven days had passed. It was the moment that I had been anxiously waiting for, the key to the first lock.

"Did you get it?" I asked excitedly after my mother answered the telephone with a business greeting.

"Yes..." she responded, with confusion in her voice.

"I'm coming over," I told her quickly and hung up the receiver, not allowing her to finish the sentence. I needed to see the report with my own eyes.

It took all of twenty minutes to reach her workplace, a janitorial supply house in the West Bronx. Entering the building through the service entrance, I wandered through an industrial labyrinth toward the office that the owner had hired my mother to manage. When I saw her face, her expression spoke of disbelief.

"It's over there," she said softly, pointing to a fax machine in the corner of that cluttered office. Advancing, I grabbed the white glossy sheet, the top page on the plastic paper tray. It was loaded with statistics, but there was one figure in particular that stood out from all the rest.

Four-point-three.

How can that be?

According to the report, Lab Five had found cocaine in my optional third sample.

Four-point-three nanograms per milligram of hair tested, to be exact.

Immediately, my mind cross-indexed my plan and my findings since my interview with the Captain and what felt like a thousand phone calls, to determine what the fax meant in the grand scheme of things.

149

Since there was a trace of cocaine in the sample, it meant that my hair was tampered with by the NYPD, and not by the California lab that had tested my first two mandatory batches.

Obviously, all three samples had been contaminated before they left the Medical Division.

However, even though logic clearly dictated that that was the only possibility, something seemed... off.

For example, the letter-sized envelope that I had mailed away with the Med Division cop in the basement of Lefrak appeared completely untampered with. Originally, the Med Division had cut my hair and sealed that third sample in front of my own eyes.

How did they manage to spike it? I asked myself.

It didn't make sense.

Obviously, I was disappointed. To have the best possible defense, I needed a clean third batch.

However, there was still a dim light at the end of the tunnel.

As previously informed, the NYPD cutoff for a positive result was five nanograms. My reading was four-point-three, a negative result by Department guidelines.

Also, there was a huge discrepancy between the three readings: Fourteen-point-one, fourteen-point-nine, and only four-point-three.

Clearly, the numbers did not match for a reason.

But what was it? And why?

I realized that I had two very important telephone calls to make, so I hugged my mother and left for home.

The first call was to Lab Five, in Chicago.

The female director was available after a short wait on hold. She seemed pleased to hear from me, quickly asking if I had received the fax.

"Yes, thank you. However, I do have some questions about the result," I said in the role of an investigator, acting impartial. "What does four-point-three nanograms mean... in layman's terms?"

"I'm not sure what you're asking," she replied, either stumped or unwilling to commit her point of view over the phone.

"Well, I have another result from the same person - taken on the same day - from another lab, a fourteen-point-nine. Is such a discrepancy... unusual?"

"Not really," she answered. "They probably utilized a different testing method, or the strands that they happened to use might have been longer. The important thing is that both labs found cocaine."

I took a deep breath and continued. "Which leads to my next question: Can a four-point-three be attributed to incidental contact?"

"Incidental contact?"

"On-the-job exposure... For instance, absorption through the skin by handling criminals, or walking through a crack den filled with smoke."

I was grasping at straws, and I knew it.

"I really don't think so," she responded apologetically. "Generally, any reading suggests drug use, even if it's only a single occasion."

"So, you're saying that a four-point-three would indicate that the subject had definitely used cocaine at least once, in... let's say, the past six months?"

"Definitely."

Thanking her through feelings of nausea, I lied and said that I would be in touch in the future.

Hanging up the receiver, it was time to contact the Medical Division.

An anonymous male cop answered the phone.

"This is Officer Ramos," I said out of habit, and began explaining my situation because I would need assistance. He cut me off mid-sentence.

"I know who you are," he replied, matter-of-factly. "Did you get the results of your third sample yet?"

"Yes," I answered hastily, unprepared for the question. The Medical Division would also receive a copy of the report, but not for a few more days via first-class mail.

"And?"

"They found a small trace of cocaine, but not enough to be considered a positive result by NYPD guidelines."

Instantly, I heard a sharp change in attitude over the line, before another word was spoken.

Regardless, there was still a purpose for the call, and I needed to stay focused.

"In any event," I continued, trying to ignore the vibe. "I need a copy of the report from the NYPD lab, regarding the first two positive results." It had occurred to me during the week that I had never asked to view the actual document for myself. For all I knew, the Captain could have invented those numbers from thin air.

"Sorry, no," he said casually, as if I had asked for a light.

"Excuse me?"

"I can't give you that."

"I don't understand."

"That report is police department property," he explained, emotionlessly. "You need a lawyer subpoena it."

"You must be kidding," I replied, with resentment in my voice. "You happen to be referring to the document that's wrongfully ending my career, and you're telling me that I have no right to see it with my own eyes?"

"Yep."

"You know what?" I began, now livid. "You claim that the results are police department property, right? Well, I am *still* a New York City police officer, which means that that piece of paper also belongs to me."

"Hold on a sec," he responded calmly, in sharp contrast. In a few moments, an authoritative female voice broke the silence.

"This is *Sergeant* Harding," she announced, putting emphasis on her rank. "What is your status, officer?"

"I am suspended without pay, ma'am."

"And you are on probation, are you not?"

"Yes, ma'am," I answered softly, my flame already extinguished.

"From where I sit, you're in no position to demand anything," she continued, condescendingly. "Now if you want the report, then I suggest that you get yourself a lawyer... Is that clear, officer?"

"Crystal."

"Oh, and another thing," she added, just before abruptly hanging up the phone. "We would appreciate it if you would stop calling our office every five minutes. You're tying up the line."

Slowly, I returned the receiver to its base, again sitting down at command central — my kitchen table — to massage my temples. Notes and numbers were sprawled across its surface, a complicated montage of winding detours and infuriating dead-ends. Struggling with an intense feeling of dread, I still couldn't afford to waste time or energy on the negative.

Soon, I would have in my possession two clean samples of hair.

And in the six days to follow, I would make arrangements with a facility in Texas that performed DNA tests, to determine the true origin of the third NYPD sample, Mr. Four-Point-Three.

Just be patient, I told myself.

It's only a matter of time, and everything will be all right.

Or so I thought.

TEN

Juan Santos was my first and only partner.

Upon my return to the 46th precinct after an interesting summer at Orchard Beach, Club Twenty-One had been replaced by a new set of recent Academy graduates, and my group had been assimilated into several traditional squads along with our elders.

Among others, Big Bird, Will Rodriguez and Tommy Pasano worked the third platoon of four-to-twelves, while Bobby Ordonez and my partner on the rape collar went to the midnight tour. Everyone in the squad had already found a suitable mate, with the exception of Juan.

Juan - or Johnny, as I liked to call him — was a strange duck. He was an ex-military guy, an uptight Semper Fi Marine machine that was a control freak, neurotic about everything within his sight or grasp.

Only five-foot-six on a slim frame, he was a heavily manicured kid who carried himself like a seven-foot giant, an obnoxious Chihuahua that could bully a Rotweiller on sheer confidence alone. It was sometimes difficult to work with him because of his intense bravado, along with a stubbornness that his way was the right way. The fact that he had found himself the odd man out on the four-to-twelve was probably not by accident.

But like a coin, there was a flip side.

157

In many ways, Johnny was a great partner.

From inside the rolling cage, the humorous social commentary that flowed nonstop from his mouth sometimes made the hours in the car feel like minutes. And with his perfect hair and good looks, he was a pure Casanova, a bona-fide woman magnet. It wasn't long before Juan had a girlfriend or two within the confines of the precinct, each taking turns cooking us Spanish pork and *pasteles* while on the clock.

But most important, he was fanatical about safety, an encyclopedia of stances and strategies, a black-belt master of verbal judo. There was not a single day on patrol that I did not feel secure in his presence, as his eyes and ears became extensions of my own.

So, five days per week, seven hours a day, Johnny and I learned about the world of the Four-Six together, from early autumn and through the bitter winter of 1998, continuing into the spring of the following year. The needs of the command dictated that we would find ourselves in a rotating sector a majority of the time, slaves to the radio inside a cramped RMP, the first pot of gold for every new patrolman.

And while cruising up and down that crime-ridden rainbow, we entered blind apartments and took turns playing shrink and marriage counselor, defusing human powder kegs and stroking fragile egos. We climbed rickety fire escapes in search of that same male in blue jeans and Timberland boots that Central claimed was responsible for every ten-ten drug sale, the violent slashings, the multiple shots fired. There were the frightening gun runs and car stops and mad dashes to help a sibling in need, to the point where the anarchy almost became routine.

Once or twice, we had the misfortune to experience that unique fear for ourselves, and we watched and cheered when the committed members of our elite gang arrived out of thin air to calm the threat.

But there were also slow nights, when Johnny and I argued like an old couple over the dumbest of topics, only to reunite once the radio sent us on a job. We would often idle and talk about our personal lives - our likes and dislikes, hopes and dreams, successes and failures, until it was time to key the portable and bid the dispatcher goodnight and go home.

And every single tour that I worked by his side, I returned to the station house to sign the roll call sheet in the exact same condition that I had left, and vice versa.

All things considered, I was fortunate to have him.

***

Two moments.

The first moment was with Johnny in a sector car, during the winter.

A new class of recruits - the second class since the release of Club Twenty-One — had been sent to the Four-Six for their FTU, flooding the streets with gray shirts hidden beneath zippered blue jackets, wide-eyed shivering statues that had not yet experienced the excitement of Madison Square Garden.

Essentially, the new kids were ordered by Four-Six supervisors to write parking tickets, listen to the radio, and just stay out of trouble.

About half-way through the tour, Central hailed our patrol car with a routine assignment.

"Six David?"

"Four-Six David," my partner answered, in his subtle Spanish accent. Johnny was invaluable to me as a translator, in an area of the Bronx that was almost seventy-percent Hispanic.

"Respond to a 10-52 - a family dispute - at two-two-seven-zero Walton, one-eight-three on the cross, apartment Four Larry on the fourth floor," the dispatcher said, reading from her monitor in a cubicle somewhere. "Complainant states that multiple people at that location are shouting loudly. Unknown weapons or injuries."

"Check and advise," Johnny replied, writing the address down inside his memo pad, before tossing the notebook into the crevasse between the dashboard and the windshield.

160

It was our ninth job of the tour, the previous eight resulting in an uneventful list of ninety-yellows, unions and zebras, police codes for false alarms. We had been aimlessly weaving in and out of quiet, one-way streets near the Deegan Expressway, so it was my guess that the trip would take about five minutes.

Suddenly, a new voice entered the car.

"Four-Six... Training One... to Central."

"Six Training One go," the dispatcher responded.

"Uh... Central, we're, um, in the area of, I mean, on foot, so... we can pick that job up... for the sector," the uneasy voice said over the frequency.

It was a bold gray, attempting to help.

"Are you a two-man foot post, Training One?" the dispatcher asked.

"Uh... yeah."

"Proceed... Six David, the foot post is handling the family dispute."

"Affirmative," Johnny replied, rolling his eyes. "Show us backing them."

Feeling apprehensive, I wiggled my portable radio off my belt, and pushed the 'talk' button.

"Central... please advise the training post to wait outside for the sector."

As predicted, it took us about five minutes to reach the low-income, six-level tenement building. As we exited the RMP and made our way inside, we hoped to see two recruits anxiously waiting in the warm lobby.

No such luck.

The elevator ride to the fourth floor felt like forever, and when the doors finally opened, we found an extremely loud woman pacing the hallway, along with twelve overwhelmed gray spectators.

Apparently, five other training teams also heard the transmission and decided to join the party.

However, not a single one — not even Training Post One — had stepped up to assume the role of leader.

They all stood around in stumped silence, paralyzed by the theatrics of the angry woman. But it was understandable - even amusing – because Johnny and I had both been there recently, as every rookie cop finds himself on the edge of that same diving board, hesitant to jump.

Like a well-oiled machine, we both went to work. The source of the woman's displeasure - her husband - was just inside the apartment, the door to 4L open wide. Immediately, I engaged with the wife, with my partner finding her mate at the threshold.

162

"Ma'am, ma'am," I said, lightly guiding her shoulder so that her body faced me and not her husband. "Don't yell. Please, talk to me. I can't help you if you won't talk to me. I want to help..."

Of course, they eventually cooled off. Thankfully, no crime was committed that evening at Four Larry - no bruises or broken bones, no weapons or unrealized threats. The duo was pure pyrotechnics, similar to dozens of other firework displays that my partner and I would witness together during my abbreviated police journey.

Before long, we had the loving couple seated calmly at the dinner table, filling out the necessary paperwork, with ten rookies watching and evaluating our tutorial.

Something special was occurring that night in the apartment, but its significance would not occur to me until we had put the job to bed and were cruising the streets once again.

When I had first arrived at the 46th precinct, our predecessors seemed like gods. When veteran cops would drive through Davidson and Jerome and West Burnside and halt their vehicles to chat with us, I was honored by their presence and hung on their every word. And if I were lucky enough to have been posted within walking distance of a job, I would rush to the location, to unleash an imaginary pen and pad, as class was about to begin.

For the first time, that night in apartment Four Larry, I saw my own eyes looking back at me.

163

The second moment was Christmas Eve, 1998.

In case you didn't realize, the New York City Police Department is never closed for business. Obviously, this is because crime doesn't sleep.

Thus, twenty-four hours a day, every single day of the year, the massive wooden portal of the Four-Six and the gates of every other command in the city are always open, even on holidays.

Roll call for the third watch at the Four-Six usually occurred at 1500 hours, or three P.M. These necessary gatherings always took place in the muster room, which was a large area on the main level of the building, a crossroads between the basement lounge, the second floor men's locker room and the vending machines. Flyers of all colors decorated the bulletin-boarded walls, detailing a wide assortment of police-related career opportunities. Brown leather couches and plastic chairs littered the edges of the room, donated by the precinct club for comfort and convenience.

However, when roll call officially began, the entry and exit doors to the sanctuary would close and everyone present would stand in respectful silence.

Normally, the sergeant assigned to roam the streets that night would adjourn the meeting. The boss would check attendance, calling out surnames against an assortment of brief responses. Then, the "Sarge" would read

164

off the tour assignments, determined in advance by the second floor civilian office workers. Finally, Sarge would finish by discussing current events, or add an occasional word of wisdom before releasing the troops.

However, this roll call would stand out from the rest, as the platoon commander decided to deliver the assignments that night, as well as voice his opinion about the year that was about to end.

"Take a quick look around you," the white-shirted Lieutenant said, pointing to the four rows of cops, about thirty total, myself included.

"The police officer standing alongside you works the busiest tour, in the busiest precinct in the Bronx - and probably the entire city. I want you to know that it has been an honor and a privilege to share the room with you... Merry Christmas."

Two moments.

Once upon a time, someone asked me a common question, to which we all have our own personal answer:

"If you had the power to change one thing from your past... What would it be?"

For a long time, my reply was to oversleep on that summer morning in 1996, when I waited outside Theodore

Roosevelt High School with a No. 2 pencil, to avoid the wasted effort, the confusion, and all the pain.

But that's not true anymore.

For those two moments, I would do it all again.

ELEVEN

My Return.

The whirlwind that swept my career away occurred four days into the pay period, which meant that my name and tax identification number was printed on the face of a small check, waiting inside a blue metal box at the Four-Six main desk.

On that unforgettable Thursday afternoon, I asked Maria to drive me to Ryer Avenue. I had in my possession a flyer of my own making, an open letter to the occupants of my second home. I figured that some cops might be curious about my situation, and I wanted to tell them in bold print that I was wrongfully accused, and fighting the good fight.

As Maria navigated the familiar fifteen-minute trip through Pelham Parkway and onto Fordham Road, I tumbled my plan of action over and over again in my head. I'd ask for the box, retrieve my check, thumbtack the flyer to a cork board in the muster room, and then quickly disappear.

The thought of cleaning out my locker had also crossed my mind, but doing so would be like giving up, a white towel thrown to the canvas.

Not yet, I told myself as my girlfriend eased into an angle spot in front of the station house.

Just get your money and go home.

When I entered the precinct, I felt as if the red stop sign at the T/S was posted for my benefit. The officer at the telephone desk, a single-hash vet, watched my approach in silence and offered a head nod, but then disappeared into a newspaper. The blue box was visible against the inside of the short metal guardrail that bordered the desk, so I leaned over and lifted the metal lid, quietly searching for my check.

At the exact moment that I located it, I felt a twenty-pound hand grab my shoulder and force me into the empty adjacent muster room.

It was none other than Frank Sumner, the Four-Six Wagonmaster.

"What the hell is going on?" he asked, in a sympathetic tone.

"I really don't know, Frank," I replied, my heartstrings beginning to tighten. "I'm trying to fight this thing."

"The whole house is in shock. People are disappointed."

Suddenly, five cops in civilian clothing entered the muster area, probably heading for the upstairs locker room.

Frank had led me away from the lobby to find some privacy, but had inadvertently placed me in the middle of the only precinct intersection.

The Fab Five were all members of Club Twenty-One, with Tommy Pasano among them.

"Hey, Chris... Did you hear what they did to us?" he said with a sad face, before seeing mine derailed his train of thought. "Uh... you okay?"

Through tense conversation, I discovered that Tommy and the quartet had been uprooted to work permanently at the Four-Eight, and weren't aware that they had been quickly upstaged for hot gossip of the week.

As traffic began to cluster around the car wreck that was my career, I gave them a skeleton version of the story, a two-minute briefing that needed two hours, maybe two days. On the surface, they seemed to side with me, offering condolences and support, probably because they had not had the opportunity to huddle up and talk amongst themselves yet, to consider the long odds, the incredulousness of my claim.

However, a small crowd of uniformed cops, both new and old, had paused to watch and listen to what must have seemed to some like the rapid-fire ramblings of an addict on the verge of self-destruction.

Big Bird was among them, glaring at me with cold eyes previously reserved only for criminals.

169

"Your locker has been clipped," the Wagonmaster said. "I think you should take a look."

Eager for an excuse to escape the scrutiny, I scrambled to the second floor, two and three steps at a time. I entered the locker room and maneuvered quickly to my private spot, a metal cabinet with my surname magic-markered on the door. My combination lock was lying on the floor nearby, the steel loop compromised by a bolt cutter.

Slowly, I opened the door to discover my belongings overturned and rifled through, many civilian items and expensive leather goods missing. It was a violation that I couldn't have imagined possible two weeks earlier.

Right then, something snapped inside me and I wept like a child, sorting through a milk crate filled with an assortment of leftovers not worthy enough to steal.

Suddenly, I realized that I was not alone.

Big Bird had followed me upstairs and stood in silence, a blue tower of curiosity. Watching my breakdown, his eyes lost their edge, making our second confrontation only slightly more bearable.

I attempted to stand tall, but my legs refused to cooperate as I slumped back down to the floor. With compassion, Kirk lifted me to my feet and was about to speak, but instead offered me a silent hug.

Many times I've wondered what Big Bird wanted to say that night in the locker room, but his restraint may have been a blessing in disguise, as it would be the remark of another familiar stranger that would be the icing on the cake, my most demoralizing moment as a cop.

But to understand how and why, I need to explain something first.

For those of you with a police background, please bear with me for a few paragraphs.

Let's say that during a random night on patrol, Johnny and I are making an arrest inside an apartment choked with narcotics.

The perp decides to resist, and during the struggle, I lose my balance and fall face-first into a pillowcase filled with cocaine.

The baggie bursts like a balloon, spraying my eyes, nose and mouth with the illegal white powder, creating an impromptu clown-face. After helping Johnny subdue the perp, I quickly wipe away the dust, and we drag our prisoner off to jail.

Now the following day, let's say I arrive at the precinct for my regularly-scheduled tour.

However, the moment that I walk through the door, the desk officer tells me to skip roll call and drive to Lefrak City, to piss in a cup.

171

I oblige, honoring the random, department-wide computer selection of my name and tax ID number, only to fail the dug test and lose my job due to an innocent, work-related incident.

But it's very easy to prevent this from happening.

Upon hauling that perp back to the command, I would immediately tell my story to the desk officer, and the scribbling boss would make a notation in the precinct diary.

Then he would give me a telephone number — as well as the page number of his entry — to tell my story again to a cop somewhere inside the walls of One Police Plaza, the headquarters of the NYPD.

More than anything else, in the event of a random drug test, that page number would save my career.

Hence the term: 'Exposure Number.'

Now, back to the Four-Six.

After I had posted the flyer, I tried to sneak away to Maria. But I had attracted a following, a small group of former peers who either wanted to have faith, or simply realized that they were witnessing a train wreck in slow motion, the first casualty of Club Twenty-One, and couldn't look away.

We migrated as a unit from the muster room out to the sidewalk across the street. Chairing the meeting, I spoke of abstracts and particulars, of logic and test discrepancies, all while fending off a mounting stampede of dishonor and shame.

And then it happened.

A single-hash vet, the same cop who had guarded the gate and delayed my entry into the Four-Six on my very first day of orientation, strolled past and uttered a loud comment while cupping his mouth with his hands, as if to mime a bullhorn.

"Get your *exposure numbers*, gentleman," he announced to the group before sitting in the passenger seat of his sector and driving off, suggesting that merely standing in my presence would be a legitimate cause for concern. "Your *exposure* numbers."

I have never been hit harder in my life.

In his understandable view, I had betrayed my oath, shit on his uniform, and risked his life and the lives of other cops by bringing an illegal habit to work and out onto dangerous streets.

To him, I would never be more than a lying hypocrite, deserving of absolutely no sympathy whatsoever.

However, none of that was the real reason why his comment hurt so much.

Here's why:

I knew that if the roles were reversed, I would've said the exact same thing.

TWELVE

Both Johnny and the mystery dog barked nonstop, filling the dying house on the hill with a cacophony of angry noise.

The condemned multifamily dwelling lived its century-long existence on the service road of the Cross Bronx Expressway, adjacent to the Four-Four. At the turn of the new year, the New York City Department of Buildings wisely decided that it was time to put the old lady down, as it was losing a battle with gravity, buckling under its own weight. The identity of the owner was another mystery, but we knew that the location had been used recently as a den for homeless squatters.

However, since the machinery of government often functioned at the pace of a garden snail, it was necessary to secure the house, to prevent some curious kid from an instantaneous burial.

Thus, every tour around the clock, two cops from the 46th precinct were assigned to babysit, to make sure it was empty.

And on one tour in 1999, when all the grays had been shipped off to guard a concert, Johnny and I got the job. Now, this would have been a simple assignment, but there was a hitch.

No RMP.

Again, the lack of a car wouldn't normally have been a big deal. Johnny and I had walked many a foot post together, and we were not above the occasional evening stroll.

However, the bitter cold of a winter that simply would not go away had wedged us firmly between a rock and a crumbling place.

That night, the temperature was easily below freezing, and with the wind chill, it made it seem below zero Fahrenheit. After only ten or fifteen minutes of exposure, the skin on my face and neck tingled and burned, making frostbite seem like a possibility.

So, our choice was clear: Suffer the effects of the brutal cold for hours, or seek refuge inside a deathtrap.

Originally, it was our plan to stay outside. But after sundown, the weather became impossible to endure. With only our flashlights for illumination, my eyes refused to adjust to the darkness. A horrid septic smell in the main level forced us up to the second floor, where we sat in a post-apocalyptic kitchen with unseen hosts scurrying about on hundreds of legs.

Johnny, our self-nominated spokesperson, blamed the platoon lieutenant, the Four-Six, the entire New York City Police Department - and even the barking dog - for being forced to make this decision.

"I'm going to fucking Florida," he said in disgust, referring to a flyer in the muster room about opportunities in the Sunshine State. "This is complete bullshit."

"Why's that?" I asked, only playing Devil's Advocate. I already knew why.

"Because we're not worth an RMP," he responded with hands flailing, his flashlight slashing through the darkness. "There are empty patrol cars just sitting in front of the station house, not being used. You saw them."

"They could have given us the day tour car," I said in agreement.

"Exactly," he said, his nostrils flaring. "This Department doesn't give a fuck about us."

Unfortunately, my partner was right. We had already asked the Lieu for a car, but had been turned down without an explanation, even though several sets of keys hung from the vehicle pegboard behind the desk.

Johnny continued.

"I'm definitely leaving. It's only a matter of time."

Suddenly, the odd mixture of barking from my partner and the mystery dog transported my mind's eye to another place and time, to the beginning of my journey. Again, I was standing at York College in business attire, shivering in formation, waiting to discover a new lifestyle.

It was time to deliver my personal pep talk to my partner and friend, the reason to endure the frustrating nights, the obscene risks, the quiet rewards.

Five and Twenty.

"Today doesn't matter. This tour is already over," I said.

"What the hell are you talking about?" he asked, looking at his wristwatch. We had at least another four hours to go.

"This job is not about any one single day. We work for the 'New York Yankees' of law enforcement agencies."

Yes, I know.

Cheesy... but I said it.

"Every true crime novel, every TV show and summer blockbuster movie — if there's a cop in it, he works for the New York City Police Department."

"That has nothing to do with us being here - tonight - in this house."

"You're wrong," I interjected, gaining momentum. "It has everything to do with it. When you raised your right hand and swore the oath, you knew the risks. You had a choice to walk away... but you didn't."

"True," he replied, his face still flustered.

"I also stayed," I continued, turning off my flashlight. My eyes had finally adjusted to the dark, metaphorical for the clarity of my happy vision. "Why? Because we have been blessed with the greatest job in the world... A front-row seat to life."

"Well... tonight sucks."

"Very true. But again, it's not about tonight. It's about the fact that in three quick years, we'll both be at a top pay that increases with every new contract. And in twenty years, you and I will still be young, with a pension and a retirement plan and a thousand stories to tell grandchildren that haven't been born yet."

I could see the enlightenment, a smile replacing the fear of falling rubble. I decided to up the ante, inviting my friend to watch a private screening, to share in my personal view of the future.

"And mark my words: I will make rank," I boasted, confident in my ability to beat any multiple choice test. I had already started studying the Patrol Guide, even though our graduating class wasn't eligible yet for the next exam. Johnny's reluctant fantasies involved the gold detective shield. "I will be a Captain someday. And when that happens, I'm dragging your ass with me to some cream puff precinct to ride out the rest of our careers — that is, if you're not busy serving warrants in a three-piece suit. We're going to laugh about this night someday — at our retirement party."

"I'm going to hold you to that," Johnny said, wagging his finger at me and grinning broadly.

"No problem," I replied, matter-of-factly, standing up to stretch. "Nothing is going to stop me from that white shirt, partner... Nothing."

With that, we decided to temporarily return to the cold and stood outside on the cracked stoop, our conversation taking a happy turn.

In the end, the building didn't fall on us, and transport would arrive only twenty minutes after the bell.

Except for the dog, I thought that we were alone that night in the house, but I should have known better.

There was a silent third party present the entire time, listening to my arrogant proclamations, a force more powerful than both God and the Devil, as deities usually deal in free will, not predestination.

It was Fate again, and he was laughing at me.

THIRTEEN

The Final Results.

Late March, 1999.

I had not seen or spoken to Johnny in about a month, a full two weeks before the roadside visit that changed my life.

We had been rudely separated on the whim of a cranky Lieutenant, as I was moved to the midnight tour without him. Conveniently, I postponed the graveyard shift by running off to IN-TAC, but had bumped into Juan once or twice in the days preceding my temporary defection. We would stop to exchange greetings, and discuss precinct and personal events.

Honestly, I had hoped to bump into him during my difficult trip to the 46th precinct station house, but his squad was off that night.

After my uncomfortable visit, I needed to talk to the only cop who would know that I was telling the truth.

The next morning, I walked to a payphone around the corner from my house, in the parking lot of a gas station. I was hesitant to dial from my cell phone or from my house, paranoid that IAB might somehow be monitoring my telephone bills, or tapping the house line.

I dumped a pocket-full of quarters on top of the metal shelf, and pushed the silver buttons.

"Hello?"

"Hey, Johnny."

"Holy shit," he exclaimed, recognizing my voice. "Chris... how the fuck have you been?"

"Not good, brother... I'm hurting real bad."

"I bet," he replied, taking a deep breath. "Listen, I gotta ask you — and I want you to tell me the truth - did you do it?"

The fact that he needed to ask was like an uppercut to the jaw.

"No."

Silence.

"You think that I did it?"

"I don't know what to think, partner," he answered, but it was a thin veil.

"How could you?" I said, revolted by his lack of faith. "It was a *scheduled* exam, Johnny. A two-year anniversary. We all knew it was coming, months in advance. I'm not stupid."

"Smart people sometimes make mistakes."

Right-left combination.

"Well... not me," I insisted, too busy grappling with shock to feel anger. "And *you* should know that."

"Why did you shave your head?"

Coincidentally, I did shave my head in December, during a trip with Maria to the Palisades Mall in upstate New York. Cringing at my thinning reflection, I asked the hairdresser to take it all off on a whim, deciding not to argue with Mother Nature any longer.

On the surface, I understood that the timing was suspicious, but I expected more from Johnny. If the Medical Division couldn't get hair from my head, then they would get it from my torso. If no chest hair, then armpit.

Regardless of a shaved head, they would get the hair they needed.

"*Think*, Johnny," I raised my voice, condescendingly. "If I had taken drugs, wouldn't I have resigned *before* the hair test? To save myself the humiliation?"

183

Silence.

"Okay," I yielded, realizing that I was talking to a blue wall. Simply put, cops believed in the test.

From the beginning, rumors about the dole exam spread like wildfire through the Academy, that the scientific analysis could trace drugs in your system back fifteen or twenty years.

Actually, it was easier than that.

Twelve hundreds cops gave hair and passed.

Johnny gave hair and passed.

But I failed.

End of story.

"Just forget it... Listen, I just wanted you to know that it was an honor to work with you."

"Likewise," he replied, sounding sincere, but then butchering his sentiment in his next breath. "Regardless of the truth, I still think you're a great guy."

"Thanks," I said, emotions shutting down. "Always be safe."

I hung up the phone, reaching into my pocket to find a piece of scratch paper. Frank Sumner had slipped me his telephone number at the station house, asking me to keep him informed.

I dropped in a few more quarters and dialed the long-distance number. A woman politely answered, and after a short delay, the Wagonmaster was on the line.

"Would that be your famous 'concubine,' Frank?" I asked him, joking but curious.

"The one and only," the big Irishman answered, chomping on something crunchy while talking. "What's going on? I want details."

"Still going strong," I said, lying. "Bugging PBA lawyers to force a hearing. Waiting for two new hair tests, to help build a case. Any day now, I should get the results that I need."

I went on to tell him about my rude conversation with the Med Division sergeant, and about Mr. Four-Point-Three. Frank listened attentively while seeming to deal with a flock of children in the background.

"Are you fighting for reinstatement?" Frank eventually asked me.

"Absolutely."

"You should resign."

"What?" I responded, stunned. "Why?"

"Even if you win, it will never be the same."

"I don't understand."

"No one will ever *trust* you," he said, pausing briefly to argue with an adolescent. After restoring order, he continued. "Everyone will think that you're a drug addict who slipped through the cracks."

"I want my life back, Frank."

"You *can't* have it back. Regardless of the reason, your former life is gone. If you resign, you might be able to get a law enforcement job in a small town, maybe in another state. But if you let them fire you from a civil service job, you'll never work for another city agency again."

"But I'm not just doing this for me," I said, thinking of the forty-thousand members of my extended family that had played the odds and won, and the few like myself that might be suffering. "If this happened to me, then it can happen to *any* cop, anywhere... Even you, Frank."

"Stop thinking like that," he scolded, trying to get me focused. "Right now, no one on my side of the fence gives a shit about you. Sorry for the bluntness, but it's the truth. All cops care about is getting a paycheck every two weeks and not getting shot at. You have to do what's best for *you* now... *Your* future."

"Can I ask you an honest question?" I said, looking to change gears. His argument made sense, but I didn't want to hear it. "Do you think that I did it?"

"That's a tough question," he said, pausing for a moment. "You're not the first cop during my time on the job to dole out. I've seen more than a few guys bring lawsuits against the Department, only to wind up arrested a few years later, buying drugs from an undercover cop."

"I'm not talking about them, Frank. I'm talking about *me*."

"I really don't know, Chris. I want to believe you. But if I had a loaded gun pointed at my head, and was told that my life depended on choosing whether you're telling the truth or lying — that if I answered correctly, I would live, but if I was wrong, the gunman would pull the trigger - I'd have to say that you did it."

"I appreciate your honesty, Frank," I heard myself saying, my brain feeling like soup.

"But what I think doesn't matter," he quickly interjected. "Only *you* know the truth. If you can look yourself in the mirror at the end of the day, that's all that matters. Do what's best for *your* life... I wish you the wisdom to make the right decision."

"Thank you," I responded, still thinking about his violent metaphor and trying to ignore his advice. Despite Frank's counsel, I still planned to fight with all my strength, win or lose.

And if I'm fired... so be it.

"Be safe, Wagonmaster."

The next morning, I was startled awake by the sound of my answering machine, recording an unfamiliar female voice. I quickly grabbed the receiver, cutting into her message in progress. It was a receptionist from the Williamsbridge doctor's office, calling to inform me that the results of my hair test had arrived from Pennsylvania, from Laboratory Number Six.

The woman refused to discuss details over the phone, insisting on an appointment with the doctor that afternoon, at three. Reluctantly, I agreed, anxiously counting down the minutes.

Upon my arrival, I was immediately ushered into an exam room, to wait alone for the physician. Sitting on the edge of the cushioned table, I was a bundle of nerves, irritated that I had been forced to wait, fearful of the implications of the telephone secrecy.

It was at that point that I noticed a beige file folder resting in a plastic bin, affixed to the door, with my surname scribbled on the outside flap.

Without hesitation, I retrieved the folder and spread the loose fax pages out on the soft table.

They were very confusing, inundated with abbreviations and medical terminology, but the verdict was clear, bolded in capital letters on the last sheet.

188

Positive.

Storming out of the office, I passed the surprised doctor in the hallway with the page firmly in my grasp, not pausing for small talk. Once in my vehicle, I dialed my mother at work.

Before I was able to talk, she informed me that our family doctor in Parkchester had already contacted her, also with a positive result from Laboratory Six.

In my mind, there was only one thing left to do.

When I returned home, I found a legal-sized envelope and addressed it to the Windy City, to Lab Five.

I brought the envelope and a piece of aluminum foil into the bathroom, grabbing my electric razor.

Removing my shirt, I studied my bare chest in the mirror for a long while, an alternating patchwork quilt of square chunks and peach fuzz, a checkerboard without the plastic chips. No longer concerned with chains of custody or contaminated samples, I shaved my chest for a final time, this test for my benefit only as the battle for reinstatement was finished, crushed under the weight of an illogical truth.

Gently, I placed the clump of hair inside the foil, and the foil inside the envelope with a money order, and mailed it away.

And a few days later, my mother received the fax, confirming the presence of the impossible.

Three-point-seven nanograms.

Somehow, the cocaine had been inside me, all along.

And with that, my spirit died.

FOURTEEN

February 26, 1999.

I received my notification slip two weeks earlier, a piece of paper that directed me to report to Lefrak on the above date, to give hair for the second time.

I had already signed off on my background check, having met with the original investigator who started my police journey in 1996.

In my mind, giving hair was just a formality. As I rode the elevator to the Medical Division on the sixteenth floor that afternoon, I thought I was already off probation, and I was happy.

Looking back, I have a difficult time remembering the exact details of that afternoon. I know that I sat in that familiar auditorium within a crowd of recognizable faces, facing that long bay window with a view of clear skies ahead. Actually, it was a comfortable reunion, with idle banter of memories from the Academy and war stories from our commands. The stand-up comedian was again present, trying to keep us both entertained and organized. They passed out empty plastic bags with bar codes, along with paperwork to fill out.

191

Among with the rest of the documents was that optional third sample sheet.

On a whim, I checked off the "yes" box.

Two years before, they scalped me. This time, I was clean-shaven, and any damage would be done to my chest, where only Maria would see.

Many times, I have wondered what my decision in the Captain's office would have been had I not shaved my head in December, had I not had a third sample.

Maybe I would have resigned, giving me an easier story to write, if at all.

But a split-second decision and a flick of the wrist changed all that, for better and for worse.

When we were done with the forms, the standing in-line began. While waiting my turn, my brand-new cellular phone began ringing on my hip. It was a new toy that I had purchased specifically for patrol, as nights and weekends were free, and that was when I wandered the precinct most.

"Honey, um... I've got a little problem."

It was Maria.

I could hear the sounds of traffic in the background, and stress in her voice.

"What is it, babe?"

"I just got into a car accident."

She gave me the details, something about a cab hitting her rear bumper. She said that she was okay, and that the collision wasn't her fault, but I had my doubts. On several occasions, I witnessed her absent-mindedly cut through three lanes of traffic to meet an exit, or slam on her brakes to avoid an already dead squirrel.

Still, if the damage was to the back of her vehicle, then she was in good shape, at least insurance-wise.

"Police report?" I asked her.

"Huh?"

"A police report... Did you have one taken yet?"

"No... should I?"

"Let me call you right back," I told her as I inched forward, one cop at a time, towards the room with the razor.

I disconnected, and called 911.

"Within the confines of the Four-Eight precinct," I told the dispatcher, slipping into my work voice. "Pelham Parkway, intersection of Southern Boulevard, between the Botanical Gardens and the Bronx Zoo. A fifty-three, two cars, unknown injuries."

"Are you at that location, sir?"

"No. Calling on behalf of a friend," I replied, giving the dispatcher Maria's cellular phone number as a callback. I thanked her for her assistance, and called Maria back.

"Stay in your car and hang tight, babe. The cops are on the way. Are you sure you're okay?"

"I think so," she answered, waffling. "My neck does hurt a little bit."

"Let EMS look at you. If they want you to go to the hospital... go."

"What would I do without you, Chris?"

"You'd find someone better."

"Not a chance... I love you."

I hung up the phone, and entered the cutting room. A black guy with dreadlocks had his shirt off, and a Med Division cop was attacking his armpit with a scissors. The same officer who would join me one month later to the post office downstairs was waiting with an electric beard trimmer. The comedian was also present, watching the action, still cracking jokes.

Ironically, I figured I'd make a few jokes of my own.

"Oh, you got me now," I said as I removed my shirt, revealing a forest of chest hair. "I should make a break for the door while I still have the chance."

"That's okay," the detective replied sarcastically, not missing an opportunity for humor. "We lower our standards for junk bags like you."

The light-hearted trash talk continued as the trimmer went to work, clumps of tainted hair falling onto a white tissue sheet. The cop made three piles, put two into clear plastic bags and the third inside a paper envelope. He sealed the packages, and I initialed all three, for verification. Afterwards, they sent me outside to the auditorium again, where I stumbled into a former company-mate, a female cop born from good-old 97-20, sitting in the front row.

We smiled at each other and quickly became nostalgic, talking about our commands and other recruits and the odd places that they had surfaced along the way. She complimented me on my new hairstyle, that it suited me.

Flattered, I thanked her, stating that Mother Nature had left me little choice in the matter.

"We made it," I said, remembering the sweaty gym marathons, the Garden sea of floating doves. "We finally made it."

"Yeah," she agreed, but then added an insightful remark. "But it's only the beginning."

And so it was.

FIFTEEN

April 2, 1999.

10 am.

It was smooth sailing on the FDR Drive that morning.

Behind the wheel driving southbound, I remember thinking that I didn't have much of a choice.

Even if the third sample had come back sparkling clean - which it didn't - in less than a week my employment with the city would be terminated, and I'd still have to sue to get a department trial.

And in that forced hearing, the judge would look at the cold hard facts: Two batches of my hair were mailed away to the most reputable drug-testing facility in the country and they both came back positive.

I had nothing concrete to fight with, and I couldn't let them fire me.

Distinctly, I remember spying other cars, as if still on patrol. I knew that I couldn't stop the future. Still, I was desperate for some form of redemption in the present, searching for some way to salvage my reputation.

As I drove downtown, I fantasized about a host of front-page headlines, something like a disgraced cop rescuing kids from a flaming wreck or from drowning in the adjacent river. It was my last opportunity to be the hero that I thought I had become on that TV screen in my head, to be deserving of the respect of my peers once more.

Of course, nothing extraordinary would happen on that drive.

Maneuvering off the exit ramp, I felt broken inside, convinced that I would never feel whole again.

The lobby of One Police Plaza was empty, except for the cop assigned to examine ID cards, reading a study guide with one eye and watching me enter with the other.

"Can I help you?" the officer asked, politely.

"I'm here to see Sergeant Russo, on the second floor."

He continued to stare, waiting for me to offer a shield, or an ID card.

"I'm suspended, sir... I have no ID."

"Name and shield number?" he asked, breaking eye contact in favor of his computer terminal. I told him the requested information, resulting in a blank screen.

"Tax ID?" he asked, apologetically.

"Nine-One-Nine-Six-Zero-One," I replied uncomfortably, giving him my city payroll number.

He typed the six digits into his terminal and waited for the supercomputer in the basement to spit back my profile.

Again, a blank screen.

"I'm sorry," the guard hastily answered, seemingly ready to show me the door. "I can't find your tax number, either."

Well, that was quick.

"Sir... I should still be in the computer. I've been suspended without pay, with disciplinary charges pending. I need to see Sergeant Russo - to resign from the Department."

Immediately, he gave me a "VISITOR" sticker, showing his decency by writing "P.O." in front of my name in magic marker. I wandered the hallways until I located the proper office and knocked on the open door.

"Sergeant Russo?" I asked.

"Yes?" the boss responded, sitting at a cluttered desk, listening to his telephone. He had thinning red hair and a beard. "Can I help you?"

"I was told by the PBA that I should speak to you... to resign."

"Give me a minute," he replied, pointing to an adjacent chair.

I sat down as instructed and eavesdropped on a pleasant conversation about golf. Directly behind him was his wall of honor, several plaques and certificates regarding specialized training. I found it very hard not to envy him, wondering not about what might have been in my career, but what should have been.

Eventually, the sergeant hung up the phone and retrieved the necessary form. After a few questions, he filled out one half of the sheet and I filled the other, making my exit official.

"If you don't mind," the supervisor began respectfully, as I was about to leave with a carbon copy. "May I ask you which drug it was?"

"Cocaine," I replied.

At that point I felt the floodgates burst open, feeling an intense need to defend myself.

"But I *didn't* do it, sir... I knew that the test was coming, months in advance."

His reply was brief, and to the point.

"Sometimes drugs make people do irrational things."

Wanting to go home and disappear, I put on a smile and thanked him. During the walk to my car, I passed a cop in the plaza area. The uniformed officer wore HQ collar brass, denoting One Police Plaza as his permanent assignment. I wished him luck in passing and he nodded silently in return.

My only thought as I drove away was that I would have given anything to wear his uniform for just one more day.

That night, I decided to return to the Four-Six, to get the rest of my belongings. My plan was to visit during the midnight tour when the house would be quiet, to attract as little attention as possible.

As expected, it was ghost town.

I bypassed the T/S officer, immediately approaching the sergeant with blinders on, not noticing a familiar person in the background.

"Sir," I began, placing the copy of my resignation on his desk. "I need to clean out my locker."

He nodded, then motioned to that unseen person. "Escort him upstairs, officer."

It was Bobby Ordonez.

As we climbed to the second floor together, Bobby spoke to fill the air, to banish any awkward silences.

"I think your locker is empty," he told me.

"They put police tape on your locker at first, to keep it sealed," he continued, trying to sugarcoat a bad situation. "Then a few days ago, the ICO vouchered your stuff. You can probably get whatever civilian items that you had when the property clerk shows up tomorrow morning."

At that moment, I realized that I would soon leave the precinct and never return.

My reputation had been stolen, my lifestyle, my detailed plan for the future.

Let them have my underwear and moldy shower shoes, I thought.

"What happened, brother?" Bobby finally asked, with sincerity in his voice.

"I don't know. I tried to fight it, Bobby..."

"You didn't do it, did you?" he stated, almost like an accusation.

"Of course not," I replied, beginning to lose my composure. "I spent money that I didn't have, trying to prove that I didn't do it. That I *couldn't*."

"Was it a set-up?" he asked.

"What?"

"Your article... in the paper," he replied, referring to an Op-Ed piece that I had written for the Daily News**, a few months before. "Maybe it was a conspiracy?"

"That doesn't make sense," I said, already having considered the possibility and discounted it. "I was supportive of the cops in that article. Besides... it's in my system."

"What.. the drugs?"

"Yeah," I affirmed, feeling my eyes go wet. "Either something that resembles drugs in a hair test, or the actual drug itself... I'll never understand it, Bobby."

At that point, I rambled on about percentage points and testing standards and trials that would never happen, my frustration growing with each breath. When I was out of air, Bobby leaned forward and hugged me tightly. Soon, the desk sergeant joined us from downstairs, probably nervous about having a jammed cop wandering his station house, on his watch.

I led them both back downstairs, and asked Bobby to follow me outside. I still had an NYPD parking plaque on my windshield, and I wanted to give it back.

"Keep it," Bobby replied, waving a finger at the neon paper that had the power to prevent parking tickets for one year, until the department would issue a different color. "You deserve that much."

"Maybe so," I answered with a half-grin, warmed by his kind words. "But it doesn't belong to me anymore."

Bobby accepted it and gave me another quick hug, saying goodbye. I watched him retreat up the steps and enter the station house, those giant doors sliding shut behind him.

Afterwards, I stood alone on the sidewalk for a long time, looking up at the brick face of the building in silence.

Suddenly, the nickname of the 46th precinct popped into my head, and I enjoyed a bitter laugh before turning away forever.

'The Alamo.'

How appropriate.

** *"See It Through Cop's Eyes,"* by Police Officer X, New York Daily News, February 14, 1998, pg. 57.

SIXTEEN

Mike was a genuine character.

I met him at IN-TAC, at the 49th precinct.

He had about fifteen years on the job, although you wouldn't have known it by his appearance. In his late thirties, Mike looked no older than twenty-seven. Italian and very handsome, he sported a tan year-round, probably because he had a full-sized tanning bed in his living room instead of a couch.

Within a half-hour of meeting Mike, he told me a detailed story about how he had been arrested in Buffalo for misdemeanor assault only two days before entering the Academy. Fifteen minutes after that, he was proudly showing me nude photographs of his beautiful wife lying on a beach during a Hedonism vacation.

It didn't take me long to realize that Mike was one of those truly blessed people who just didn't care what people thought of him, and that included his supervisors.

In fact, Mike had been shipped off to IN-TAC by an XO that had grown tired of being called 'fuckface' on a regular basis.

As insane as Mike obviously was, he was also a funny guy, with a natural magnetism that made him difficult not to like.

Somehow, I became his shadow for my two weeks at the Four-Nine.

Shortly before I left the Four-Six, I discovered that the midnight tour was not my cup of tea.

Instantly, I felt like a zombie. The tour began at eleven PM, running until seven in the morning. Normally, I was alert until about three AM, but then came a brick wall. After that, I would push through until I got my second wind, making it impossible to fall asleep. My constitution fought that bizarre schedule, instantly resulting in pale skin, dark circles, and constipation.

Then, from out of nowhere, 'Cookie' saved me.

Cookie was the nickname for a female cop at the Alamo who came out of the Academy six months before me.

I had no clue about the origin of her nickname, and I never asked. She was Hispanic with a trace of an accent, with blonde curly hair and a slender frame. We never really spoke at the command, besides polite hello-goodbye greetings in the muster room.

Yet, it was her bruised English on the line when my telephone rang on a day off.

"I'm looking for someone to hold a spot for me," she said.

"What does that mean?"

205

"I'm at the Four-Nine," she answered, explaining her recent disappearance from the house. "I'm working in a training detail. I need someone to hold my spot."

Obviously, I was still confused. "What are you doing over there, exactly?"

"It's great... You work from noon to eight, no patrol. Civilian clothing, all day. You play a criminal in scenarios, training cops. Y'know... acting."

Immediately, I saw the pot of gold. The Four-Nine was only five minutes from my house, maybe three from Maria's. But there had to be a hole in the rainbow.

"Well, if it's *so* great... Why are you leaving?"

"I'm not," she replied, sounding wounded. "You're only allowed to stay for one month at a time. If I can find a cop from the Four-Six to hold my spot, then when your month is over, I'm allowed to go back. Honestly, I love it here."

Needless to say, I accepted Cookie's offer. When my three-day weekend concluded, I was off to IN-TAC for what I believed would be a month of fun and relaxation, and the detail did its best to hold up its end of the bargain.

Like Orchard Beach, I would roll out of bed at noon for roll call, this time in a cluttered office with Mike and a dozen other cops on the second floor of the police precinct on Eastchester Road. Until three o'clock, we would waste time reading the paper and eating egg sandwiches, watching daytime soap operas and Blockbuster video tapes.

Then, at three-thirty, the real fun would begin.

For outdoor scenes, we would all jam into a police van and head down to the adjacent Jacobi Hospital parking lot, to borrow a quiet corner and create car stop situations. A crowd of Bronx patrolmen would meet us in the lot in full uniform, taking turns as our guinea pigs.

At the end of several training scenarios, we would all cluster in a huddle and discuss the good, the bad and the ugly. After that, we would all retreat into an empty theater on hospital grounds to act out a few family disputes.

Mike was by far the best actor in the group. During an indoor scene, I remember him cowering in fear under his seat in the auditorium, wailing like a baby when a 'gunfight' broke out in a crowded movie theater. On another occasion, he played a suicidal off-duty cop, brandishing a fake pistol with irreverence, venting frustration over career and broken relationships.

On a memorable afternoon that he had played a restaurant owner, I discovered that Mike had plenty of real life experience.

"I'm also a *Maître 'D*," he explained.

Coincidentally, we had many of the same civilian acquaintances, including Fred in the pizzeria and Robert waiting tables in the same restaurant where Mike worked off-duty.

"Small world," I said.

The following day, Mike and I made an unannounced visit to order food for the IN-TAC crew. The employees at the restaurant were well-accustomed to random visits from both of us, but never together.

Our temporary partnership came as a shock to some, as Mike and I had conflicting reputations: I was Mr. Goody-Two-Shoes, while he was considered a lunatic.

"You better stay away from that guy," Fred said to me jokingly, smiling from a sauce-stained apron. "He'll get you into trouble."

Actually, Mike never had the opportunity.

I had only three days left.

***

It was like any other day.

I woke up at eleven-thirty and threw on some civilian clothing, shoving my backup revolver into a fanny pack and grabbing an NFL highlight tape on the way out the door. Since I knew that there wouldn't be any Bronx cops arriving at the Four-Nine for training that day, I figured that the video would be a good way to kill some time.

My short drive was peaceful, finding a great parking spot directly across the street from the precinct. I signed the in-sheet upstairs at noon, said hello to Mike and a few others and found a comfortable couch to 'vege' out on for a few hours. Maria called me on my cellular phone to tell me not to eat heavily, that she planned to have Chinese for both of us that evening. I thanked her for the food and everything else, and then read the newspaper from cover to cover, sports section first, like always.

At about one-thirty, the group settled on McDonald's for lunch, and I volunteered to make the trip. After making a list, I grabbed the keys to the big police van that we used for training. On my way past the Four-Nine desk, I stumbled into a familiar face from the recent past.

It was one of the boat cops, from Orchard Beach.

He looked a bit odd dressed in full uniform, having worn only a blue t-shirt and dark shorts for the summer.

I stopped briefly to chat and reminisce, genuinely happy to see him.

"Are you returning to the beach this summer?" I remember him asking me.

"Uh... sure," I replied, not expecting the question.

"Well... Tim is up for sergeant. He's not coming back," the boat cop explained, referring to his other half. "I'm probably going to need a new partner on the water. You've been out with us... I'll put in a good word for you."

As I sat in the driver's seat of the van outside, I thought to myself how flattering his offer had been. I had made friends at Orchard, and a large majority would be returning again. Much like the other places that I had worked, there was a comforting sense of family at the Beach.

Yeah, I said to myself as I randomly picked up a batch of printed sheets from the floor of the messy vehicle, held together by a small metal staple. *I'm definitely going back.*

Upon closer inspection, I realized that it was a personnel order, a type of memo that chronicles all the movement within the NYPD, with lists of names and tax identification numbers.

The first few pages regarded promotions of every level - from patrolman to detective or sergeant, all the way up to captain and beyond - plus their new commands. Curiously, I flipped through the pages, to see if I recognized any of the names.

In the back of my mind, I imagined my own name listed in a future memo, having already begun studying the Patrol Guide for future exams.

Not finding any familiar names, I was just about to toss the papers aside, but then the last page grabbed my attention.

Almost like the epilogue to a story, there was a short list with only three names on it, each officer with a tax number from my own graduating class. Tragically, all three had failed their end-of-probation dole exams due to the presence of illegal drugs, each terminated from the Department as per their zero-tolerance policy.

Examining the names, I searched my memory for a white or sky-blue t-shirt running laps in the Academy gym, to match a name to a face.

Again, no such luck.

I tossed the memo aside, much like the NYPD had done to its three bad apples.

Poor idiots, I thought to myself, unaware of the impending irony.

And my final day as a police officer continued, just like any other.

SEVENTEEN

Samson and Delilah.

A story of a man, a woman, and a deception.

There is a loss of power, associated with the loss of hair.

Vaguely, I remember helping my father restore the backyard deck of our house on a quiet Sunday afternoon, about two weeks after my resignation at One Police Plaza.

The wooden foundation of the deck screamed for repair, worn from multiple seasons of exposure to the elements. Dad had always been a handyman, at peace in his tool shed with all of his assorted hammers and drill bits. Usually, I opted out of such projects, but I badly needed a distraction, and that was at least half of his reason for requesting my help. Surrounded by boxes of nails and piles of weather-treated lumber, I was able to keep my body occupied as my subconscious continued to wrestle with the only question left that mattered in the grand scheme of things.

Soon, I would learn that my father had already developed a theory, and felt the need to share.

On a soda break, he sat me down for a private conversation.

212

"How do you think it happened?"

I could only shrug my shoulders.

"Have you ever asked Maria if she's used cocaine?"

Immediately, I didn't like where the conversation was heading. Maria had been my rock through it all, a shoulder to lean on throughout my difficult ordeal.

"Yes, I did... A long time ago."

"And?"

"She told me that she's never done it."

"Not *ever*? Not even before she met you?"

"I asked her about drugs at the beginning of our relationship," I continued, uneasy with the subject but trying to hide it. If she did the drug, he seemed to be saying, then maybe you did the drug with her.

However, I would soon find out that I was jumping to the wrong conclusion.

"I had made it clear to her, Dad - from Day One — that we wouldn't be together if she dabbled in anything illegal."

"Y'know..." Dad began, heading off on a tangent that would officially pry open Pandora's Box forever. "At your sister's wedding, I noticed that Maria went with Rena into the bathroom... twice."

Rena was a friend of the family, a fifty-something Arthur Avenue Italian lady who was a fixture at every family function, to the point that I had adopted her as my aunt even though we weren't actually related. From appearances, she was the stereotypical mob-wife-slash-girlfriend-on-the-side with the big teased hair and mink coat, reminding me of the redhead Ginger from the old TV serial 'Gilligan's Island.'

"Where are you going with this, Dad?"

"Well... Rena uses coke."

"Really?" I responded, not sure if I actually knew or not, but not really caring. After all, Aunt Rena's habits were her own, and I had never witnessed anything personally. "So?"

"That doesn't seem odd to you?"

I was rapidly losing patience. "Dad... It's common for women to go to the bathroom together. It's not that big of a deal."

"I think it is."

"I told you that I didn't do coke," I said.

"I didn't say that you did, son."

"Then what are you saying?"

"How long have you and Maria been having sex?"

It was a bold question, but not shocking. We had discussed my sexual encounters throughout the years, my relationship with Maria included. He was only asking to illustrate his point. "For more than a year."

"Isn't it possible that she passed a trace of the drug from her body into yours?"

Honestly, the idea had crossed my mind, but I quickly discounted it. I had been faithful, and I knew for a fact that Maria did not do drugs. In our time spent together, she had displayed none of the trademark 'cokehead' signs: bulging eyeballs, eighty-five-miles-per-hour conversations, and a jaw that wiggled like a vibrator. Besides, I wasn't even sure if transmission by such means was a possibility.

"So, you're suggesting that she passed cocaine from her body into mine... through sex?" I asked him, incredulously. "That's nonsense. It's not even proven."

"Maybe so," he admitted, but continued his line of reasoning, his intensity growing. "But let's forget about sex for a minute. Let's say that one day Maria had decided to use coke. She snorts a few lines, licks the inside of the bag for the residue, and brushes her teeth with her finger. You stroll into her apartment and shove your tongue down her throat. You don't have to be a doctor to know that the cocaine is still in her saliva and on her gums. You exchanged bodily fluids with that woman on a regular basis for more than a year. If she used drugs on a regular basis, then so did you."

"But she never used drugs, Dad. I would have seen it..."

"Love is blind, my son," he said, using an old cliché that fit well, considering the circumstances.

That evening, I drove to Maria's house, for dinner. We ate, watched a movie, made love. There was an angry little man yelling in the pit of my stomach, but I couldn't hear him clearly, at least not yet.

She was disappointed when I refused to spend the night, asking if there was anything wrong. I said that I didn't feel well, which wasn't a lie.

On the way home, I decided to stop at Fred's house. His basement was filled with friends like always, people drinking beer and listening to music, among other things.

Like before, I sat down on an empty chair next to Fred in his bedroom, as he watched sports highlights on the TV. I closed the door behind me, wanting privacy.

"My father thinks that it's Maria's fault," I said.

"Funny you should mention that," Fred replied, pressing the 'mute' button on the remote. "That's pretty much what we think, too."

"We?" I asked, surprised.

216

"It's still a hot topic. We discussed it for about an hour yesterday... Only the regulars."

"And?"

"Well, we know *you* didn't do it," Fred said, putting out a half-finished hand-rolled marijuana cigarette, saving it for later in his ashtray. "But we think that *she* did."

"Why do you say that?"

He took a deep breath. "Well, six months ago, you and Maria came into the pizzeria. I was working, and so was Rob. The boss and his friend were also at the counter... Remember?"

"Yeah," I replied, not sure if I did but eager to advance the story.

"When you and Maria left, the boss' friend asked if Maria was your girlfriend. We told him yes. He rolled his eyes and said that she was 'bad news.'"

The little voice inside me started screaming again. Ignoring it, I let Fred continue.

"He went on to tell a story about Maria and two guys in a local bar, about a year ago. He said that she did coke with them in the bathroom. Supposedly, one of the two guys was the owner's son."

There was a long silence. When the bitterness finally cleared from my throat, I spoke. "You heard this story six months ago?"

"Yes."

"Who else knows about it?"

"Pretty much everybody."

Again, silence followed. Fred lit a cigarette and began flipping through the TV channels. Simmering, I looked at the marijuana roach in his ashtray and had an urge to relight it and take a hit. *Why not?* I thought to myself. There would be no more tests to take, nothing left to prove to anyone.

Except to myself.

"Do you think that the story is true?"

"I really don't know," Fred answered, locking eyes with me before neatly summing up his opinion. "But if it is... it certainly would explain things."

Too much, too fast. As I lay in bed trying to sleep that night, I could hear the fury of that twisted little voice again, spouting convincing arguments against the woman that I loved. Fortunately, I had no time to think, as I had to somehow clear my head and hold a heavy camera on my shoulder the following day. The world would not wait for my recovery, and working part-time as a videographer was a way to pay a few bills.

218

It was a small wedding reception, a check in exchange for pressing a little red 'REC' button and keeping the woman in the white dress in frame and in focus. Piece of cake, except that the *Maître D'* at the catering hall happened to be Mike, from IN-TAC.

"What about your girlfriend?" Mike asked after he had pulled me aside and I yapped at length about the past month. "Isn't she a known drug user?"

"Excuse me?" I replied, shocked. "Who told you that?"

"Let's just say it's not much of a secret."

"Mike, I really need to know," I continued, desperate for more than just rumors. "As far as I know, she's clean."

He paused and gave me a dubious stare. "Look, I'm not going to lie to your face and then talk shit about you behind your back. You're a good guy, and you deserve better than that. Maybe you ate coke off of her pussy, for all I care... It's your business, and I won't think badly of you, either way."

Mike then proceeded to share a story about when he smuggled cocaine inside his underwear through customs upon returning from a vacation in Jamaica, while he was a police officer. As he joked about fooling a German Shepherd at the airport, there was a piece of me that sincerely respected his honesty.

However, the rest of me wanted to bounce his bronzed forehead off the dance floor.

Off-duty or not, he was a cop and I wasn't, so I listened politely and pressed the little red button until I was able to retreat to Maria's house in a very sour mood.

That night, while lying in bed next to my sleeping girlfriend, I finally decided to listen to that angry little man in my stomach.

"She's a cokehead, and a liar," the voice said.

"How do you figure? There are no signs."

"Are you kidding? Just because her jaw doesn't shake? Don't be an idiot."

I looked over at Maria with adjusted eyes. She was asleep on her side and facing me, snoring. Her face was flawless, even with crazy bedroom hair and no makeup. "No, not my Maria. She would never hurt me."

"*Really*?" he replied, the word drenched with sarcasm. "What about Orchard Beach?"

Low-blow. The two-week hiccup in our relationship, her betrayal that I had forgiven, or at least forgotten. "That was different... She did that for her kids."

"She did that for her*self*," my cynical side scolded, picking at an old scab. "It was an opportunity for her to get her old life back. Of course, she wanted to be with her kids.

She also wanted the house and the lifestyle to which she had been accustomed. If it was only about her children, then she could have brought them down to the Bronx, to live with her. "

About that, I couldn't argue. I had never completely understood why she chose to leave Newburgh without her boys. According to Maria, to make them live in the Bronx would have been too disruptive, that her husband was better able to provide a good life for them upstate. It almost made sense.

Then again, to another woman in her shoes, the decision to leave her kids behind with a physically abusive man would have been unimaginable.

Suddenly, a flash photo of Nick appeared inside my head, standing in the alley during our confrontation, calm and composed. He wasn't exactly the callous and manipulative beast that I had heard so much about. Maybe he was nothing more than an ordinary man who loved his wife, despite many hard lessons learned.

"So... she uses?"

"Ever since the first day that she met you, in that diner. And deep down, you knew the truth. You just didn't care. As long as she gave you what you wanted - attention, love, *sex* - nothing else mattered."

In the beginning of our relationship, I had given her an ultimatum, practically forcing her to lie to keep me. If she had honestly admitted her habit, I would have walked away. Both flattered by her decision to live a lie and disturbed by my own stupidity, there was still one thing left to understand. "Why hasn't she come out of the closet now, after everything that's happened?"

"Maybe if you could take the bad news with a grain of salt and just start your life over, then she'd be able to come clean," the voice said. "But Maria knows that if she told the truth, you would expect - no, *demand* - that she go to war for your reinstatement, to step up and announce to the whole world that she's a cokehead, that it was *her* fault that you lost your job. Besides the embarrassment to her family, it would have a huge impact on her divorce. Obviously, she must have done something illegal for a judge to award full custody to her husband. If she were to admit in a hearing that she used illegal drugs, then he could use that to keep her kids away from her, citing that she's an unfit mother. And in the end, you'd leave her anyway, because the whole relationship was based on a lie, from the beginning."

Again, I glanced over at the sleeping woman lying next to me. For the first time since fate had arranged our introduction, I finally saw the person that I had been cursed to love with my eyes wide open.

I saw Delilah.

"Don't you dare put all the blame on her shoulders," the voice said.

"Why not? I didn't do it... She did."

"*You* had a chance to fix things, at the Beach. After telling you that she would love you forever, she left a cowardly *Dear John* letter on the windshield of your car, and then came crawling back only two weeks later. She betrayed you, and you took her back... So, in the end, it's *your* fault."

"Sweetie," Maria suddenly purred through the darkness, half-asleep and reaching out, running her palm over my patchwork quilt of chest hair, the testing ground. "Did you say something?"

"No," I whispered softly, unaware that I had been talking out loud. "Go back to sleep, honey."

And she did. Eventually I also fell asleep, but not before staring at her for a long while, wondering what to do. I still loved her, even if I knew that our relationship was doomed.

That week, I said and did nothing, but tried to avoid the ringing of the telephone. Maria could tell that something was wrong, but I couldn't find the right words until I had a chance to talk to Aunt Rena, while she was visiting my grandmother in the upstairs apartment of my three-family house.

"I'm so sorry what happened to you," Rena said when I pulled her into an adjacent room, to talk privately. "A damn shame."

"Thanks," I responded, almost afraid to proceed. "I need to ask you something."

"Go ahead."

"At the wedding... I noticed that you and Maria went into the bathroom together," I said, hinting at the obvious. "Did you and her..."

"No," Rena interrupted, mid-sentence. "She fixed her makeup and talked about how much she loves you. I went into one of the stalls, by myself. Had she knocked on the door, I would've shared... But she didn't."

"Please," I pleaded, desperate for some kind of confirmation. This would be my best opportunity. "I really need to know."

"I know your situation," she said in a convincing manner. "If she had used with me that night, I would've confronted her, and told her to tell you the truth... But she didn't."

Disappointed, I stood up to leave... and then she said it.

"But she's *definitely* used coke before."

I sat back down.

"That's not what she told me."

"Oh, that's a lie," she replied, matter-of-factly. "It's easy to hide from people that don't use. Actually, I've had boyfriends for years that had no idea."

224

With a specific plan in mind, I went back downstairs and entered the bathroom. Looking for my razor, I found a pair of scissors instead, realizing that Mom's hairdressing cutters would be better suited for the task ahead. After that, I found an envelope in a clutter drawer, and lined the inside with foil.

Then, I left and drove to Maria's apartment to determine the truth, once and for all.

I knew from an earlier voicemail that she was out shopping with her mother, so I opened the door with my key and settled into my favorite chair, a suede recliner, and awaited her return.

After a short wait, Maria appeared with two grocery bags, smiling over my unexpected visit. It was a warm afternoon for April, and she wore a clingy sundress that accented her shapely figure. Even in my frenzied state, she was beautiful and always would be, at least in my eyes.

However, it was time for her to step up to the plate for the man she loved.

"Honey, I need you to do something for me."

And so began a fierce debate, resulting in her refusal to take the test.

Her reasoning was sound: I had failed the dole exam, and she chose to believe.

225

According to her, I needed to take that same leap of faith.

So, I left her apartment that afternoon without the proof I needed.

We had not yet said goodbye to each other, but the damage was already done.

However - despite being convinced of her guilt - I would soon discover that there was still one more possibility.

EIGHTEEN

My story ends where it began - at the Academy.

On the final day of my career, the Lieutenant at IN-TAC sent me and two other cops to that tall building in Manhattan, to ascend to the sixth floor to make dummy rounds for the fake yellow-barrel revolvers.

At about four o'clock, we scrambled into the van in our civilian clothing and made that twenty-plus minute ride downtown via the FDR, traffic permitting. There was no timetable for our trip, as long as we returned to the Four-Nine with two huge coffee cans filled with fake bullets before the end of tour. While traffic did slow down our progress, it made really no difference. We were free to roam the streets, basically New York City royalty on a mission from the king of the IN-TAC castle.

Upon entering the Academy, I again read the message above the spinning threshold that had always brought a smile to my face:

For 150 years, the Finest cops in the world have passed through these doors...

RESPECT AND UPHOLD THAT TRADITION!

Walking beneath that decal-on-glass sign towards the inner stairwell, I was reminded of the sense of pride that I felt on the Garden floor at graduation, the white doves and the explosion of applause that followed.

Nothing in the world could compare to that moment, frozen in time.

Instead of ascending immediately to the sixth floor, one of us came up with a great idea. Once per month, every cop was allowed to waste a box of real ammunition in the firing range in the basement, so we decided to descend into the sub-level to locate the men in khaki uniforms, hoping to load up and blast away.

Unfortunately, the shooting range was closed on that particular afternoon, and there was a long line of gray shirts on the verge of receiving their guns for the very first time, another class of rookies about to embark on their field training.

Not until many weeks later would the irony of that moment hit me like a brick to the face.

I realized that I had been standing at a kind of crossroads, walking past an excited group and traveling in the opposite direction.

As their careers were about to begin, mine was about to end.

Disappointed by our poor timing, we jumped on the elevator and pushed button number six. Upon reaching the floor, someone in blue directed us to a series of closets at the end of a long corridor. We quickly found the proper door, and dragged the coffee-grinder-looking-contraption out into the hallway.

Having no clue how to operate the device, Randy and Ray crushed their noodles together to try to figure it out. As too many cooks often spoil the brew, I ventured off on a personal quest, to find the Police Science office.

When I was a young gray, I noticed that other members of my company had laminated their memo book inserts, the pages of radio codes held in their leather binders, as the sheets were required for patrol. Back then, I thought that it was overkill, but time and use had ravaged my own inserts, causing more than a few to fall out and disappear.

Even though I had memorized most of the codes, it seemed like a good idea to get replacements, as I fully expected to be returning to patrol in two weeks.

So, I got my new inserts and returned to the hallway. By then, my comrades had the process down to a science, cranking out the dummies, rapid-fire.

After that, we left the Academy to roam, eventually finding a highway that would lead us back to the Bronx.

During the return trip, I looked at my wristwatch.

Eighteen-hundred hours, on an exceptionally cold day, even for March.

And my novel began.

NINETEEN

On a random day in July, my mother brought home a photocopy that was given to her by a co-worker, who was married to a Bronx cop. It was a copy of a department memo,** direct from One Police Plaza, mailed and faxed to every command across the city.

This particular Patrol Guide amendment was filled with complex legal terminology, but its primary purpose was clear, at least to me.

Undoubtedly, the subject matter would become the answer to a future test question, on a Saturday morning promotional exam:

There are certain foods, spices, oils, body sprays, hair care and beauty products, prescription and over-the-counter medicines that may give you a false positive on an NYPD drug test.

There is no way to know which products will do this, as most ingredient labels will probably neglect to mention the presence of such substances.

However, none of that matters, if you do fail.

Consider this a fair warning.

If you fail a department dole test, regardless of how you may or may not have been exposed, you will be fired.

If you don't like it, go find another job.

After reading it, I called my lawyer.

"There's really not much that you can do," he calmly advised me during my umpteenth free telephone consultation. A friend of the family, and a good man.

"How is that possible? The NYPD is admitting that their drug test is inaccurate, that a false result is a possibility. How can I not have a case?"

"Well... you resigned."

"But... I had no choice," I said in my defense. "The drug was *in* my system. Waiting for the department to fire me would have been stupid."

"Your resignation could also be construed as an admission of guilt," he pointed out.

It was a double-edged sword. Resign, and you must be guilty. But let them fire you, and it's future career suicide. My lawyer continued. "Plus, you'd still have to force the department to grant you a trial, with no guarantee of the outcome. That would take thousands of dollars in legal fees. And remember: You still have no evidence that you didn't put the drug into your body intentionally."

232

Like many times before, I thanked him and hung up the phone.

Long after finally putting this subject matter to bed and moving on with my life, it's that damn memo that still burns me.

** NYPD Memo: PG 104 Series, Number 37, Date Issued: 7-19-99.

***

The engagement party.

It was a special night, to celebrate the upcoming marriage of two close friends, a joyous occasion for everyone invited to the catered event. It was also a perfect excuse to put all the recent events temporarily aside and just have fun, for at least one night.

But as much as I wanted to forget and enjoy myself, I couldn't.

After reading the memo, a weight had been lifted off my shoulders, allowing me to feel love for Maria again. With an alternate explanation that made sense, I wanted to return to our previous path, of a wedding someday of our own.

But the glass had already been broken, and no piece of paper was going to repair the damage.

A few days before the party, she confessed that she had already met someone else.

Instead of going to the party alone, I asked her to stand by my side for one more night, secretly hoping for an opportunity to somehow turn the tide. She honored my request and sat with me like always, but as we drove to the catering hall, I could feel an invisible wall in the car, keeping us apart.

In the end, I would lose both loves of my life, and I felt powerless to stop any of it.

So, with Maria both within reach and a thousand miles away, I watched two happy people take center stage under the glow of the multicolored DJ lamps. Much like a wedding itself, there were toasts and dedications, slow-dances with parents, even a cake-cutting ceremony. When appropriate, I clapped in unison with the hands around me, quietly daydreaming of a time machine that could send me back to my sister's wedding, four days before the roadside visit by IAB, the last perfect day. At my sister's reception, I clapped for real as Maria and I danced and drank the night rotten, without a worry in the world.

Feeling empty inside, I didn't just want the party to end.

That night, I was seriously thinking of ending it all.

Luckily for me, I saw a familiar face in the crowd, a cop's face.

It was John D'Angelo, from York College.

John approached with a handshake, followed by a warm hug. Still a monster of a man, he again barely fit inside his suit jacket, with that same thick face and round shoulders that seemed even bigger since our days at orientation.

Our first meeting since my incident, it was impossible not to remember our private talk in the lunchroom long ago, how I had played God with his life and his career. And after all the cards were laid on the table, it was I that was pulled from the group instead, humiliated and tarnished, just as he had secretly feared for himself.

Choking on the irony, I made an awkward attempt to explain the unexplainable, fighting that familiar sense of shame that made no sense, but still followed me like a shadow. But he would interrupt my plea, with words that would help me enjoy the rest of the night.

"Chris," he said with honest eyes.

"You don't have to defend yourself... I *know*."

And with that, I began to heal.

***

It is a good analogy, almost perfect.

Imagine that one day you wake up to find that you have wings, and that you can fly.

Now, you never wanted to fly, never even considered the possibility. At first, the experience is awkward, even frightening. After all, birds and insects fly, not people.

However, as time goes by, you become more confident with your new ability and you use your wings often, eventually almost forgetting how to walk.

These wings allow you to see life from a new perspective that you never thought possible, from the clouds above. And before long, you can't imagine your life without them. They become as much a part of you as your legs, your eyes, even your heart.

Then, after a few years, you wake up to discover that your wings are gone, as if they had never existed.

Eventually, the shock and hurt will subside, but there is not a single day thereafter that you don't reach a curious hand behind your back or look over your shoulder in a mirror, to wish for what you know you will never have again.

With each step, I still look to the sky and dream.

ABOUT THE AUTHOR

Robbin Ramos is a child of New York City and a graduate of Lehman College, where he was honored with membership in Phi Beta Kappa and won awards for journalism and fiction writing.

Regarding the NYPD, Robbin is extremely proud of his experience as a cop, and he wouldn't give it back for the world.

Currently, he is married and lives in Hartsdale, New York.

Made in the USA
Middletown, DE
19 April 2022